IMAGES
of America

NEW FAIRFIELD

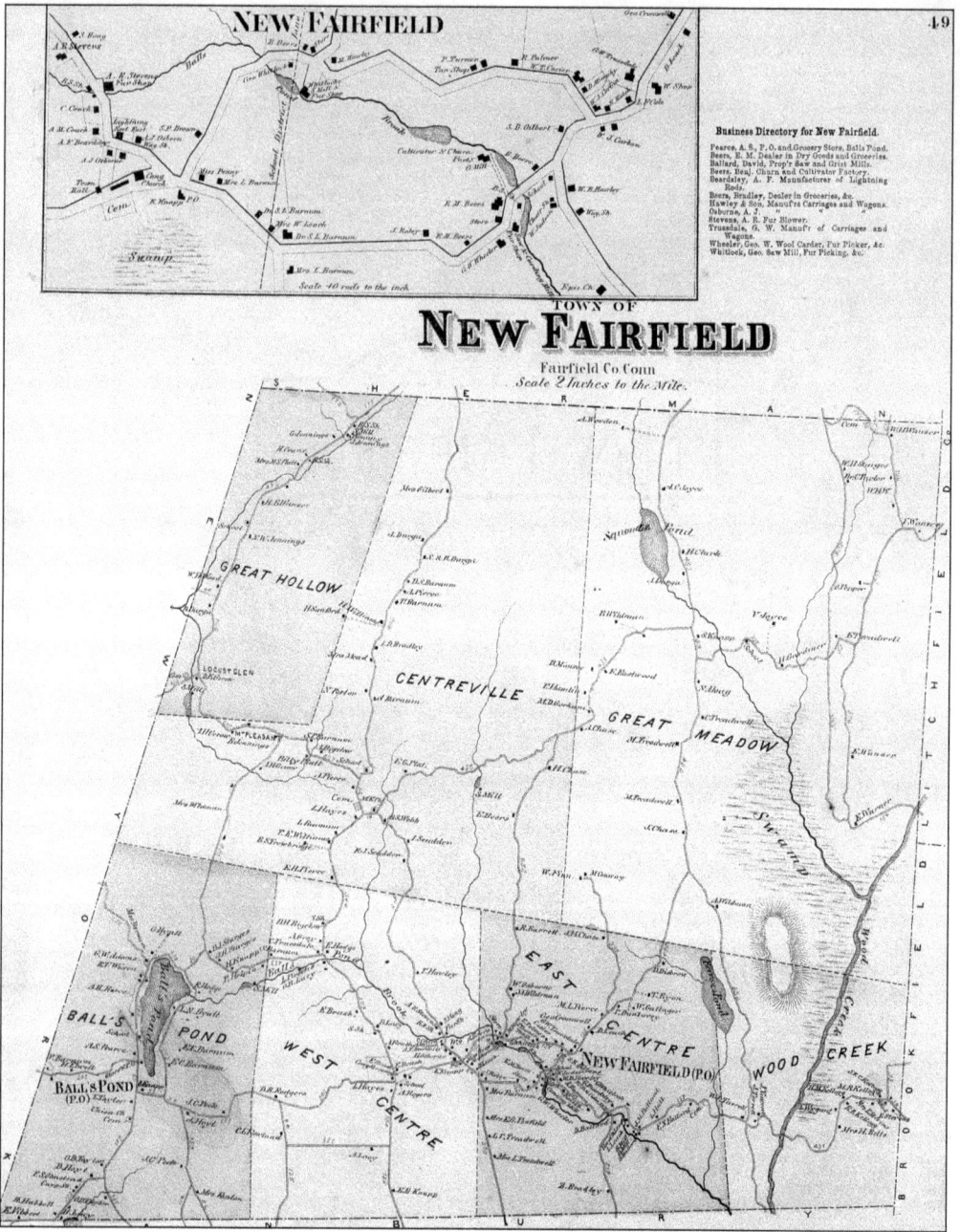

TOWN OF
NEW FAIRFIELD
Fairfield Co. Conn
Scale 2 Inches to the Mile.

Business Directory for New Fairfield.

Pearce, A. S., P. O. and Grocery Store, Balls Pond.
Beers, E. M. Dealer in Dry Goods and Groceries.
Ballard, David, Prop'r Saw and Grist Mills.
Beers, Benj. Churn and Cultivator Factory.
Beardsley, A. F. Manufacturer of Lightning Rods.
Beers, Bradley, Dealer in Groceries, &c.
Hawley & Son, Manuf'rs Carriages and Wagons.
Osburne, A. J.   "
Stevens, A. R. Fur Blower.
Trusdale, G. W. Manuf'r of Carriages and Wagons.
Wheeler, Geo. W. Wool Carder, Fur Picker, &c.
Whitlock, Geo. Saw Mill, Fur Picking, &c.

BEERS MAP. Seen here is the 1867 Beers map of New Fairfield.

On the cover: **TOWN HALL, 1934.** On June 9, 1934, town residents celebrated the opening of an addition on the east side of the original 1759 town hall building that housed an auditorium. This was a much needed space for square dances, wedding receptions, firemen's Christmas parties, and town meetings. This space now functions as a probate court, selectman's office, tax collector's, and town assessor's office. (Courtesy of Janice Zackeo.)

IMAGES
of America

NEW FAIRFIELD

Preserve New Fairfield, Inc.

ARCADIA
PUBLISHING

Published by Arcadia Publishing
Charleston SC, Chicago IL, Portsmouth NH, San Francisco CA

Library of Congress Catalog Card Number: 2007939810

For all general information contact Arcadia Publishing at:
Telephone 843-853-2070
Fax 843-853-0044
E-mail sales@arcadiapublishing.com
For customer service and orders:
Toll-Free 1-888-313-2665

Visit us on the Internet at www.arcadiapublishing.com

This book is dedicated to the people of the town of New Fairfield.
"A nation with no regard for its past, has little hope for the future."

CONTENTS

ACKNOWLEDGMENTS

Preserve New Fairfield, Inc. wishes to thank the many people who worked so hard to make this book possible, including Doug Barrios, Richard Bessel Jr., Hazel and Willie Burger, Barbara Hawley Coelho, Alfred Colo, Community Service Club of New Fairfield, Congregational Church of New Fairfield, Leonard Copicotto, Joseph Coniglio, Joyce Czudak, Linda Decker, Lloyd Decker, Ellen Fecci, Robert Fox, Daniel and Marion Gerow, John and Genevieve Gilbert, Anthony and Marie Gillotti, James Green, Michael Halas, Donald and Judy Hatch, Ruth Kaeser Hawley, Michael and Dottie Hess, John Hodge, Richard and Millie Johnson, Ken Kellogg, William McCann, Helen Middleton, Alex Monshaw, David Monshaw, Susan Monshaw, Harry and Joanne Moody, John D. and Joan Muir, New Fairfield Historical Society, New Fairfield Community Parks and Recreation office, New Fairfield Community Thrift Shop, New Fairfield Public Library, Sue Ann Newton, Donald Novicky, James Ogden, Diana Peck, Jessica Plate, Karen Schermeister, Susan Spaulding, Richard Sturm, Irving Straiton, Susan Sulich, Betty Swan, Kenneth Taylor, Klaus and Wally Theil, Agnes Betty Trimpert, Alex Thomson, Craig Wright, and Janice Zackeo.

INTRODUCTION

It is so easy to drive past historic buildings and hardly notice them. Of course, if they are grandly restored, or crumbling into a pile, they call attention to themselves. Otherwise, they sit silently, witnessing the many changes that occur in a town over time. Often these changes go unnoticed by the people living there, but the houses can tell stories of days past and the fascinating events of a small town with a big history.

New Fairfield is exactly that sort of small town. Though few famous people have lived here and few headlines have been made, this charming little corner of Connecticut is rich with the stories of change that tell a true American tale. From sprawling agricultural roots to a time of surprisingly diverse industry to today's commuting culture, the sense of home for those who live here has changed very little indeed.

In 1729, after years of negotiation, the sons of Chief Squantz, leader of the Schaticooke tribe, sold the 30,000 acres of swamp and hills comprising the town to a group of men from Fairfield known as the proprietors. The price at the time was 65 pounds sterling, or about $300. The original property contained what was commonly called "the upper seven miles," today's town of Sherman (1802), and the "lower seven miles," the present-day town of New Fairfield.

The Congregational Church played a very big part in early New Fairfield history. In addition to its ecclesiastical role, it was also the center of government and social and educational life. Built in 1742, the church satisfied the need for "the existence of a meeting house," for the town to become incorporated. Later the town leaders felt that the government should separate from the church, so the town hall was built in 1759 and an independent governing body was formed.

The A. Beardsley home, on what is now old Route 37, was purchased by the Congregational Church in 1903 to be the parsonage for the minister and his family. It was recently saved from demolition, moved to a new location, and today operates as a local history museum. The Greek Revival–era home continues to tell its story of the meetings, social events, Sunday school lessons, and family gatherings that took place within its walls. This once silent building now has a loud voice in sharing the history of the town.

Water has been a continuing theme of importance in New Fairfield's story. Sawmills and gristmills dotted the landscape in the 19th century as enterprising residents made very good use of the various streams running throughout the countryside. Ball Pond was once a popular spot to bring the family for a relaxing vacation at one of the small hotels and inns sitting near the water's edge or to rent a cabin on the opposite shore near Weldon Woods.

In the northern portion of town on the edge of the Pootatuck Forest, Squantz Pond was a great place for camping, picnicking, canoeing, fishing, and swimming. In 1933, the federal government installed a Civilian Conservation Corps (CCC) camp there to help relieve mounting unemployment pressures due to the Great Depression. The Squantz Pond State Park today remains an important natural resource and a very popular summertime destination.

The star of the show, of course, is magnificent Candlewood Lake. Considered to be an engineering wonder, the lake was designed to provide much-needed hydroelectric power to this growing region. The Connecticut Light and Power Company took advantage of a series of small ponds and large, swampy regions feeding into the Housatonic and Rocky Rivers and flooded the valley to control the flow of water.

Construction of the lake began in 1926 and was controversial, as some longtime residents were forced to sell family property to make way for the flooding of the valley. Cemeteries were moved, houses and barns were knocked down, and thousands of trees were felled to make way for what became the largest man-made lake in the state and one of the largest in the country. In the following decades, many waterfront summer communities were built and today serve as year-round residences.

Candlewood Lake gets it name from the early local Native American practice of taking thin strips of wood from the heart of a pine tree and using it as kindling for fires. New Fairfield boasts more lakefront property than the other four towns (Brookfield, Danbury, New Milford, and Sherman) that share Candlewood's shores. There is a great park for town residents, featuring two beaches and a marina for boats.

While New Fairfield has maintained a small-town atmosphere, it has been steadily growing. Census numbers were at their lowest in 1938, with only 434 permanent residents. By the end of the 20th century, those numbers swelled to more than 12,000 people calling New Fairfield home.

In the early days of public education, the town was divided into seven districts, each one serving a group of children who walked to a small, one-room schoolhouse. These districts included West Centre, Great Hollow, Wood Creek, Ball Pond, East Centre, Great Meadow, and Centreville. Typically the buildings were heated by a wood-burning stove and had no running water. The children carried water in buckets from a nearby pump and an outhouse was available, even in winter snow. In 1830, the teacher at Ball Pond School earned a salary of $10 per month plus board. Each family provided a sufficient amount of firewood and a new broom at the start of each school year on October 1.

The one-room schoolhouses closed by 1941, and the Consolidated School opened. Transportation was provided by school buses, often station wagons. The empty, old buildings were converted to private homes or torn down. However, one remains standing as a schoolhouse. It is the West Centre School, which was restored and is used by the New Fairfield Historical Society to show modern school children what life was like in the "good old days" of ink wells, woolen mittens, and dunce caps.

The 1867 Beers map of New Fairfield, seen on page 2, is an excellent historical resource and it shows a surprisingly diverse number of industries flourishing at that time. Sprinkled about the center of town were a churn and cultivator factory, a manufacturer of lightening rods, and a carriage-building shop. There were also fur and wool processing factories that supplied the hat-making industry in neighboring Danbury. Small dry goods and grocery stores offered the essentials, but it was more than a century before a supermarket in town eliminated the need for a weekly, out-of-town shopping trip.

The industries may be gone, the way of life may have changed, and new faces have replaced the old, but the same community spirit is very much alive in this beautiful New England town.

One

GONE BUT NOT FORGOTTEN

OCTOBER HOUSE, 1947. Located on the 1867 Beers map of New Fairfield at the intersection of what is now Route 37 and Saw Mill Road, this home was built by David Barnum in October 1771. Later it became well known as the home of Bruce Rogers (1925–1957), world famous typographer and book designer. The home was razed in 1989. The original structure was actually the middle portion as pictured here. (Courtesy of New Fairfield Free Public Library.)

OLIVER TAYLOR HOMESTEAD, 1864. Built for Oliver Taylor's bride, Valeria Pearce, this magnificent home is said to have been a replica of a French chateau. The home stood on the corner of what is now Route 39 and Milltown Road and burned down in 1945. (Courtesy of Lloyd and Linda Decker.)

SEELIG'S HOTEL POSTCARD, C. 1905. Once standing on what is now Ball Pond Road East, this farmhouse attracted city dwellers looking for a bit of rest and relaxation. One of the many diversions offered was a "twilight stroll." (Courtesy of New Fairfield Historical Society.)

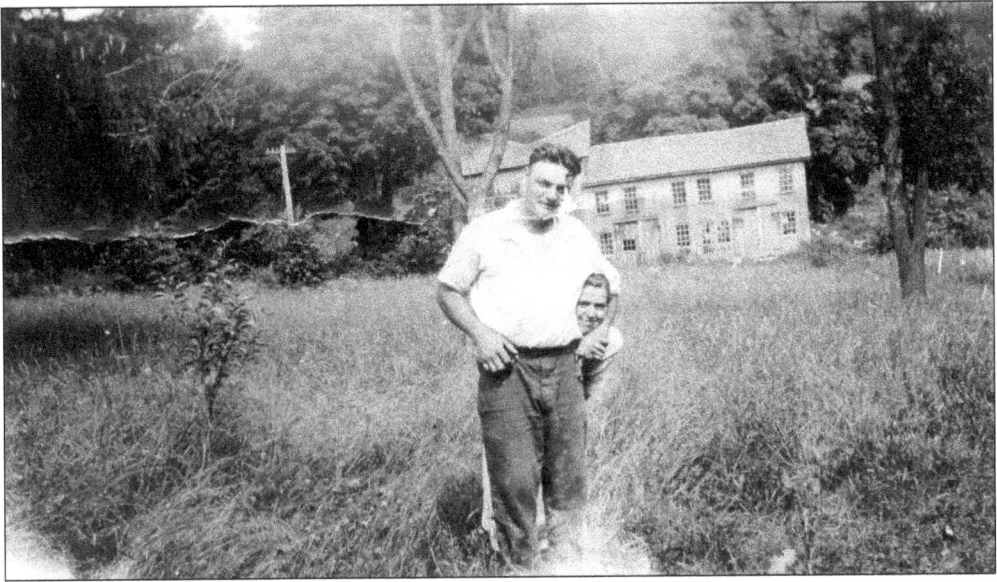

BLACKSMITH SHOP, 1917. As the need for horseshoes and hand-forged farm tools was diminishing, Ernest Benedict converted his business to carpentry. Pictured here is Ken Joyce, a carpenter's apprentice, and his wife, Sarah Benedict. (Courtesy of Preserve New Fairfield, Inc.)

EMILY BROWN'S BARN, 1945. Noted for its unique several-story height, this barn stood on the property that is now Union Savings Bank near the intersection of Route 37 and Route 39. Emily Brown was famous for taking on the job of tax collector when her husband, Frank, died suddenly in 1932. She retired in 1960 at the age of 88. (Courtesy of New Fairfield Free Public Library.)

CHATTERTON FARM, 1920. This was one of the many established farms claimed by the flooding and subsequent creation of Candlewood Lake in 1926. Located just beyond the town park on what is now Knollcrest, descendents of the family today run a successful boat marina on the bit of property that remains above water. (Courtesy of Leonard Copicotto.)

DANBURY FAIR, 1924. Henry Horberg and Elizabeth Donaldson join friends and neighbors at the much-anticipated annual Danbury Fair. Begun as an agricultural exhibition in late 1800s, the popular event closed in 1981, making way for today's shopping mall. In its heyday, fairgoers could see horse races, automobile races, boat races, Victor Zombroski's orchestra, the fat lady on the midway, and a re-creation of a Dutch village. (Courtesy of Kenneth Taylor.)

DAYTON HOMESTEAD, 1900. Here are Henry and Lottie Dayton in the yard of their home, once located on Route 37 between Saw Mill and Cottontail Roads. This house is listed on the 1867 Beers map of New Fairfield as belonging to Dr. S. L. Barnum. Henry was famous for his dandelion wine. (Courtesy of New Fairfield Free Public Library.)

JOYCELAND FILLING STATION, 1938. Virginia, Lillian, and Ellen pose before the pumps that dispensed gasoline at a price of 10¢ per gallon. (Courtesy of Leonard Copicotto.)

BALL POND OBELISK, 1900. This ancient stone structure stood just north of what is now Ilion Road on the west side of Ball Pond. It was said to have been there before the Native Americans. It was approximately seven feet high. (Courtesy of New Fairfield Historical Society.)

14

MEADOWBROOK PLAYHOUSE, 1965. Built by Russ Dunham and John Kizarr, the theater opened its doors in July with *Bye, Bye Birdie*. A capacity crowd sporting black ties and mink stoles cheered, though the stage lacked a curtain, backdrop, and lighting. The name changed to Candlewood Theatre later that year. During its lifetime it was host to local productions such as *90 Minutes from Broadway*, concerts, and recitals. Some big names stomped those boards, including Jerry Lewis and Barry Manilow. (Courtesy of New Fairfield Historical Society.)

MARTHA POST FAIRCHILD HOME, 1970. Having been the Post family homestead for generations, it is the scene of Martha Post Fairchild's "Red Rambler Rose" memoirs. She had a great recollection of the gardens and "putting up" foods for winter use. The property was owned by the Turner family on the 1867 Beers map of New Fairfield. (Courtesy of New Fairfield Historical Society.)

CHASE FARM, 1940s. Brothers Arthur and Edwin Chase are bringing in hay on their farm, which was located at the intersection of Routes 37 and 39, where the New Fairfield Shopping Center is today. (Courtesy of Lloyd and Linda Decker.)

DISBROW BARN, 1920. This photograph was taken from the west side of Route 37 where Margerie Reservoir is today. These barns were taken down before the land was flooded in 1934 to create the reservoir. The swampy area served as cranberry bogs. It was reported that a wagon and horses were lost to quicksand there. (Courtesy of Harry and Joanne Moody.)

WOODCREEK POSTCARD, 1907. This was the main road to Brookfield, linking the two communities, until the land was flooded to create Candlewood Lake. New Fairfield's Apple Trees section ended up on the opposite shore. (Courtesy of Preserve New Fairfield, Inc.)

GEROW FARM, 1924. The sawmill in the foreground on the right was in operation until its demolition in the early 1990s. The ice house in the background at left was one of many in town. (Courtesy of Daniel and Marion Gerow.)

Two

COWS AND COMMERCE

BARNS IN THE CENTER OF TOWN, LATE 1940S. Brothers Arthur (left) and Edwin Chase cross Route 37 after putting their cows out to pasture on property that today is a gas station. Notice the large, metal milk cans standing at the far left. The farmhouse is now the Village Hardware Store. (Courtesy of New Fairfield Historical Society.)

COWS ON "S" ROAD, 1920. Located on what is today known as Gillotti Road, the stone house was built in 1915 by Jane Schermerhorn and still stands today adjacent to the high school property. (Courtesy of Klaus and Wally Theil.)

PRIZE BULL, 1930s. Arthur L. Disbrow admires his prize-winning bull. His brother Lewis Disbrow is in the background. (Courtesy of Harry and Joanne Moody.)

HOMER NORTON, 1930S. Sporting a Danbury hat, Homer Norton poses with one of his milk cows. The hill in the background was later known as Oakwood Acres; today it is Rita Drive, behind Company A firehouse. (Courtesy of Donald Novicky.)

DISBROW FARM, 1920. From left to right, little Phil Pinckney, Hazel Hatch Pinckney holding Buddy Pinckney, Bessie Nevius Bigelow holding and son Donald, and Phebe Disbrow Moody holding son Harry enjoy a play date. The farm, located on Route 37, became the Possum Ridge development. (Courtesy of Harry and Joanne Moody.)

HALAS DAIRY DELIVERY, 1950. Paul Halas delivers milk to New Fairfield customers from his 148-acre family farm on Bear Mountain Road. Other companies offering regular home delivery included Watkins Products (spices, salves), Dugan Bakery, Rider Dairy, and Locust Hill Farm (eggs). (Courtesy of Michael Halas.)

COWS COME HOME, 1920S. A large herd grazes in the pasture of the Disbrow farm. The open land in the background is the northeast corner of Possum Ridge today. (Courtesy of Harry and Joanne Moody.)

Rocky Fields, 1916. Sometimes called "Connecticut potatoes," rocks in the cornfield on Bear Mountain Road made hoeing difficult for George Benedict (left) and hired hand Mr. Brown and his dog, Felix. (Courtesy of Preserve New Fairfield, Inc.)

Sheep Farming, 1921. In New Fairfield, and throughout New England, the practice of keeping sheep diminished in the early part of the 20th century as the price of wool dropped and the cost of keeping the animals rose. (Courtesy of Donald and Judy Hatch.)

HATCH CARRIAGE FACTORY, 1921. The building stands today on Candlewood Corners, previously known as Millers Corner, then Hatch's Corner. Hatch Carriage Factory, established in 1855, built several styles from city-going phaetons to utility farm wagons. (Courtesy of Donald and Judy Hatch.)

COMMERCE AT CANDLEWOOD CORNERS, 1960S. Around 1960, the Little Cake Box Bakery shared the building with James Camarata's package store and Collins-Morrow Real Estate, the developer of Charcoal Ridge, Smoke Hill, and other subdivisions. If it looks familiar, the Community Thrift Shop and *Citizen News* are there now. (Courtesy of New Fairfield Historical Society.)

GATHERING TOBACCO, 1918. Tobacco growing was prevalent as early as the 1880s and continued to be a cash crop until the early 1900s in New Fairfield. It was said that one could get a loan based upon projected crop growth, then priced at an average of 10¢ per pound. (Courtesy of Preserve New Fairfield, Inc.)

HUBBELL HOUSE, C. 1840. One of the earliest inhabitants of this old house was Revolutionary War pensioner Gideon Hubbell. The little building served as a post office in the 1880s. It lived on in the 20th century as a newspaper office, antique and gift shop, paperback book exchange, and ceramic studio. A country store filled the outbuilding for many years. Today, the house has been moved from its original site and serves as a local history museum. (Courtesy of Preserve New Fairfield, Inc.)

FILLING THE SILO AT DISBROW FARM, 1920s. Notice the amount of equipment and horsepower necessary to get this job done. A lot of manpower was required to fill the silos with chopped corn. Weather permitting, farms could expect to harvest two crops of hay during the summer months. (Courtesy of Harry and Joanne Moody.)

RUMLEY TRACTION ENGINE, 1920s. This type of traction engine was used on many farms of the early 1900s. (Courtesy of Harry and Joanne Moody.)

PICKING UP HAY AT THE DISBROW FARM, 1920S. The woman and young girl pictured in this photograph may have just brought lunch to the men working the farm. The land seen in the background is now Possum Ridge. (Courtesy of Harry and Joanne Moody.)

SNOW-COVERED HAYSTACKS, 1940S. This homemade farm equipment on the Gillotti farm rests in front of two large haystacks. Hay was harvested in the summer and used throughout the winter for many things, including insulation. This land is now part of Komlo Field. (Courtesy of Anthony and Marie Gillotti.)

LAKESIDE FARM, 1905. Once a prime summer resort on Ball Pond Road East, this hot spot attracted visitors from as far away as New York City. (Courtesy of Janice Zackeo.)

CASH AND CARRY ICE, 1930s. The roadside icehouse was a frequent stop for visitors to the lake and for summer travelers. The business was run by Walter Czudak Sr. in the 1930s. (Courtesy of Walter Czudak family.)

JOHNSON FARM, 1940s. This is a typical scene found around New Fairfield in the 1940s. The barn in the background was part of Johnson's farm, which was located on Route 37. (Courtesy of Richard and Millie Johnson.)

CUTTING ICE ON BALL POND, 1925. The Hatch men cut and loaded ice to sell to local businesses and families. The ice was cut in wintertime, covered with sawdust, and placed into buildings that were also insulated with sawdust. This ice lasted throughout the summer, cooling milk and other dairy products. (Courtesy of New Fairfield Historical Society.)

BACKER FARM, 1910–1913. The Backer Family Farm, on what is now known as Turtle Bay, was once one of New Fairfield's largest farms. The original town road ran between the house, which later burned down, and the barn. Presently, New Fairfield Town Park is located just beyond the barn. (Courtesy of Richard Sturm.)

BACKER FARM WITH TELEPHONE, 1910–1913. Long after the flooding of Candlewood Lake, the barn on the right was relocated and became a residence. Beginning with two-party lines, telephone service came to the area about six years before this photograph was taken. Five lines were in the center of town, and three were located near Ball's Pond. (Courtesy of Richard Sturm.)

BACKER BARN, 1910–1913. The baby, Adam Krauser, is being held by his aunt and uncle on Backer farm. The road in front of the barn is the Old Town Road, which was later moved to make way for the flooding of Candlewood Lake. Today it is Route 39. (Courtesy of Richard Sturm.)

BACKER FARM AND SHORELINE, 1910–1913. The open field located at the top of this photograph is the Candlewood Isle shoreline. Today Candlewood Isle is one of New Fairfield's largest private communities. (Courtesy of Richard Sturm.)

LANDSCAPE VIEW OF BACKER FARM, 1910–1913. Backer farm was originally owned by Jacob and Martha Backer and later operated by Henry and Mary Backer. Henry held the office of selectman in New Fairfield in the early 1900s. (Courtesy of Richard Sturm.)

BACKER BARN AND RESIDENCE, 1910–1913. The farm was well-known for its production of tobacco, hay, and milk for the residents of New Fairfield and surrounding towns. The 1898 tax list indicates that, at the time, Jacob Backer owned 301 acres of land. (Courtesy of Richard Sturm.)

LOOKING NORTH ALONG ROUTE 37, 1940S. This photograph was taken from the front porch of the Johnson farmhouse. Originally owned by Henry Johnson, it was a gas station and the Surrey Light Snack bar. It became a popular gathering place for New Fairfield's youth. Today the location is still used for commercial purposes. (Courtesy of Richard and Millie Johnson.)

RAKING HAY, 1940S. Richard Bessel Sr. is shown raking hay on the family farm on Pine Hill Road. Of the many farms that were located on Pine Hill Road in the early 1900s, only the Rywalt farm still exists today. (Courtesy of Richard and Lee Bessel, Jr.)

GREEN LIGHT RESTAURANT, 1948. Notice the 1936 Ford parked in front of this popular eating spot. For over 60 years, this location has been home to several eating establishments, serving local residents and visiting tourists. (Courtesy of Hazel and Willie Burger.)

CANDLEWOOD ISLE TRADING POST, 1940s. This structure still houses a post office as it did back in the 1940s, as well as a local realty office. It serves the Candlewood Isle community. (Courtesy New Fairfield Free Public Library.)

CAMP HOOK, 1933–1935. The Civilian Conservation Corps (CCC), which established a site located in Pootatuck State Forest, left a legacy of hiking trails and fire roads. Starting out as tents, these were later transformed into barracks that housed the many unemployed young men who joined the CCC to learn to swing an ax, chop wood, and hone their building skills. (Courtesy of Leonard Copicotto.)

MEN WORKING, 1933–1935. Under Pres. Franklin D. Roosevelt's New Deal, which was established to battle the depressed economy, these men worked to help raise money for their families. They received $30 per month, $25 of which was sent home and $5 of which they could keep for themselves. (Courtesy of Leonard Copicotto.)

35

CUTTING WOOD, 1941. Arthur Chase and Byron Foster are shown cutting wood that was used for heating homes and cooking. Located at the intersections of Routes 37 and 39, it is now home to the New Fairfield Shopping Center. (Courtesy of New Fairfield Historical Society.)

CAUSEWAY LUMBER, 1950S. Causeway Lumber, the supplier for the 1950s housing boom, was located in the converted farmhouse of Arthur and Georgiana Chase. The building was moved slightly to accommodate the development of the New Fairfield Shopping Center. On the 1867 Beers map of New Fairfield, it is listed as the Knapp place. The Village Hardware Store is now located in the building. (Courtesy of New Fairfield Historical Society.)

Three

AROUND THE TOWN

SNOWPLOWING ON ELWELL ROAD, 1930. Local men cleared the roads with their own equipment, charging the town for their work. Here Edison Elwell drives his team to the end of Elwell Road opposite the intersection of Warwick Road and Route 39. He earned $55 for the winter of 1910. (Courtesy of Preserve New Fairfield, Inc.)

MAILBOXES ON BOGUS HILL, 1954. "Neither snow nor sleet" deters the mail delivery in New Fairfield. In 1869, the mail carrier came to town only twice a week from Danbury. In 1959, New Fairfield opened its own post office. (Courtesy of Willie and Hazel Burger.)

FRANK BAILEY, MAIL CARRIER, 1910. A popular figure on his route number 19, which took him to the town center, Frank Bailey returned to Danbury after making his rounds and brought with him eggs and produce from people on his route. (Courtesy of Preserve New Fairfield, Inc.)

NEW FAIRFIELD TOWN HALL, 1920. Built in 1759, the building had a stone vault added after a fire destroyed town records kept at the home of the town clerk in 1867. In 1896, the Sons of New Fairfield voted to install a town library in the lobby where books rested on shelves behind glass. (Photograph by E. H. Pearce; courtesy Leonard Copicotto.)

TOWN CENTER, C. 1900. Pictured from left to right are the Couch house; the Hubbell house; the Beardsley house, which is today the Parsonage; the town hall with its stone vault; carriage sheds for churchgoers; and the Congregational Church, which burned in 1921. Houses on the left side were on what is now Route 37 heading north. Note the New Fairfield Cemetery in the foreground. (Courtesy of Leonard Copicotto.)

JOYCELAND TOURIST HOME, 1927. This popular vacation spot was situated on Squantz Pond. When excavations began for this building (still standing today), an entire skeleton was unearthed, believed to be Chief Squantz resting in his camping ground. Keith Joyce also found arrowheads, tomahawks, and other implements on the property. (Courtesy of Leonard Copicotto.)

CAMPER AT JOYCELAND, 1932. This is the beginning of recreational vehicles. Note the 1932 automobile in the yard. (Courtesy of Leonard Copicotto.)

40

JOYCELAND CABIN, 1930. Built on the shores of Squantz Pond in 1929, Joyceland offered holiday-goers a manor house with a dance hall and casino, cabins, and water sports. Notice the washing machine on the right side of the porch. (Courtesy of Leonard Copicotto.)

KNOLLCREST, 1940S. Fred Fuchs digs out after a snowstorm on Chatterton Point. The windmill behind him never functioned as a mill, but the building has served as a meeting place and offices for the Knollcrest Residents' Association. (Courtesy of John and Genevieve Gilbert.)

High Ground near Candlewood Lake, Early 1930s. Cousins pose with the family automobile. From left to right are Robert Joyce, Rose Joyce, Mary Joyce, and Ruth Chatterton. (Courtesy of Leonard Copicotto.)

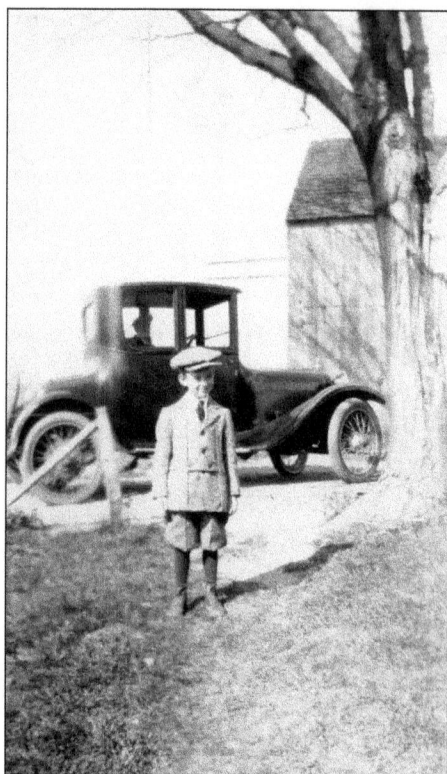

Sunday Drive, Early 1920s. Not yet old enough to wear long pants, five-year-old Harry Moody is ready to take a spin in his dad's Dodge. (Courtesy of Harry and Joanne Moody.)

PINE HILL, 1920. Howard Sanford remembers getting telephone service here in 1914, years before electricity came to town. It was necessary to put a nickel in the telephone to get it to work; it ran on a dry-cell battery. A representative of the telephone company came to empty the nickels and replace the battery periodically. (Courtesy of Preserve New Fairfield, Inc.)

SUGAR AND SPICE, 1950S. Little girls have not changed much over the years. Here Janet Morgan (left) and Jane Ruppell tend to their dollies on the Disbrow farm. (Courtesy of Harry and Joanne Moody.)

CANDLEWOOD LAKE IN DISTANCE, 1920S. Looking down the hill from the Johnston home on Saw Mill Road, one could see the commercial district on the far left and the Wheeler house. The two houses in the foreground are no longer standing. (Courtesy of James Green.)

KNOLLCREST WINDMILL, 1936. The well-known Candlewood Lake landmark was intended to pump water for the new Knollcrest development, but it never drew a drop. Damage from a 1938 hurricane spurred the first of many renovations of the 80-foot-tall structure. (Courtesy of New Fairfield Free Public Library.)

HAZEL HATCH PINCKNEY, 1916. Hazel Hatch Pinckney was one of the first local girls to get a driver's license. (Courtesy of Donald and Judy Hatch.)

NEW FAIRFIELD'S FINEST, 1972. Joseph Hubert, state trooper Robert Rosen, Thomas McLoughlin, and Frank Sacco pose with their Plymouth squad cars in front of the New Fairfield Library. An addition to the building was built right on this spot in 1975. (Courtesy of Lloyd and Linda Decker.)

GOING TO THE MARKET, 1950. With no supermarket in town, Dorothea Fox is seen in this Fox family photograph loading her Jeep to the First National grocery store (now the site of the Danbury *News-Times* newspaper) on Main Street, Danbury, for her weekly shopping. (Courtesy of the Fox family.)

FIAT CAR, 1927. Elizabeth Donaldson perches on Henry Horberg's car. He notes on the back of the photograph, "This is my car the Fiat. Ask the boys if they would like to ride 65 or 70 miles an hour in it. The Fairchilds thought it was an airplane when they heard it coming." (Courtesy of Kenneth Taylor.)

46

Four

WATER'S EDGE

ICEBOATING, 1930S. Water activities have always been an important part of life in New Fairfield. Year-round on the shores of Candlewood Lake, Squantz Pond, Ball Pond, and various streams, residents have enjoyed a variety of recreation. The sport of iceboating rivaled that of ice fishing as a popular pastime in the 1930s. A good breeze could sail a boat from Knollcrest right down to the Danbury town park. (Courtesy of New Fairfield Free Public Library.)

BALL POND HOTEL, 1940s. Here is a picturesque view of the Ball Pond Hotel complex from the water's edge. The hotel, built in the 1920s, provided rest and relaxation for many summer visitors who vacationed in New Fairfield. (Courtesy of John D. and Joan Muir.)

COUNCIL ROCK, 1915. Offering sweeping views of the Squantz Pond valley, a hike through the Pootatuck Forest to Council Rock conjures images of Native American tribes, including Scatacook, Waramaug, and Pauguasett, traveling to their ancient, regional meeting place. (Courtesy of Leonard Copicotto.)

BEFORE THE BUILDING BOOM, 1936. The Taylor family enjoys a picnic at the top of what is today Escape Road off Wood Creek Road. Esther Taylor and her son Kenneth are joined by Esther Thorell and Emma Horberg. Sweetcake Mountain is on the left, Hollywyle is on the right, and Candlewood Lake is in the distance. (Courtesy of Kenneth Taylor.)

NATURAL BEAUTY, 1948. These lovely ladies pose on a dock with Squantz Pond State Park on the opposite shore. They were probably contestants in the Miss Candlewood Lake beauty pageant held at Joyceland. (Courtesy of Leonard Copicotto.)

BEACH AT BALL POND HOTEL, C. 1966. Susan Muir and Linda Sheehan lived near the Ball Pond Hotel and enjoyed its beach and ice-cream stand. It was safe to walk along the road and buy a soda at the hotel, they recall. (Courtesy of John D. and Joan Muir.)

DIRT ROAD, WOODEN GUARD RAILS, C. 1900. The Benjamin Yale blacksmith shop stands in the far right of this photograph that shows the intersection of Ball Pond Road East and Route 39. (Courtesy of New Fairfield Historical Society.)

EARLY LAKESIDE CABIN, 1930s. This cabin, with a fabulous view from Overlook Drive, is very typical of the first homes built in the lakeside communities of Candlewood Knolls and Candlewood Isle. Strict regulations called for specific siding materials and paint colors. (Courtesy of James and Melissa Ogden.)

OUTBOARD RACES, 1940s. Among its many organized activities, the Candlewood Knolls community sponsored motorboat races. Though the races are no longer formally held, many local boaters like to race along the open waters of Candlewood Lake. (Courtesy of New Fairfield Free Public Library.)

THE LIVING IS EASY, JULY 1944. Boating was just one of the many pleasant ways to pass a summer's day at Squantz Pond State Park. Camping was popular from 1944 until it was discontinued in 1964. (Courtesy of Leonard Copicotto.)

LIFEGUARDS, 1963. Employed by the Town of New Fairfield, these brave swimmers watched the beaches at the Candlewood Town Park and Ball Pond. The lifeguard posts were on a rotating basis. From left to right are (first row) Bob Coniglio, Karen Schermeister, and Finn Gulbrandson; (second row) Mark Wolmer, John Gulbrandson, and Dick Mills. (Courtesy of Karen Schermeister.)

BIRD'S-EYE VIEW OF KNOLLCREST, 1940S. Notice the famous windmill in the center of this photograph. Compared to today, there are few houses that dot this spit of land surrounded by Candlewood Lake. (Courtesy of New Fairfield Free Public Library.)

CIVILIAN CONSERVATION CORPS BARRACKS, 1933. Wooden buildings were erected south of Shortwoods Road to house the men who were employed by the CCC work program implemented by Pres. Franklin D. Roosevelt. Designed to ease financial hardship during the Great Depression, the New Fairfield crews built roads, developed a nature trail, and helped with snow removal. (Courtesy of Leonard Copicotto.)

PORTABLE COTTAGE, 1938. Muir family members Elsie, Alan, and John pose before their 1927 Chevrolet touring car and summer bungalow on Satterlee Road. This unique, small building was put together with latches and bolts in four-by-four sections. The front was added on later. (Courtesy of John D. and Joan Muir.)

MISS TWIGGLEY'S TREE, 1950S. The willow branches framing this Fox family photograph of Dorothea Fox and her children Bob and Becky belong to Miss Twiggley's tree, the subject of Dorothea's famous children's book published in 1966. (Courtesy of New Fairfield Historical Society.)

SUNDAY VISTA, 1950S. John Muir and a cousin enjoy the magnificent view of Squantz Pond from Shortwoods Road. (Courtesy of John D. and Joan Muir.)

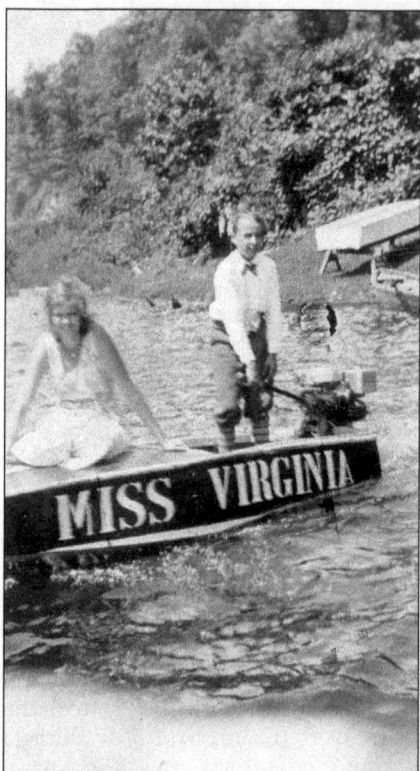

MOTORBOATING, 1931. Pictured at age 15, Virginia Faubel and a companion take a spin in her namesake on Squantz Pond. (Courtesy of Leonard Copicotto.)

ICE HOCKEY, 1940S. No pads, no helmets, no penalty box—these people play ice hockey with just sticks and skates on Candlewood Lake. (Courtesy of New Fairfield Free Public Library.)

SKATING NEAR THE CAUSEWAY, 1950S. Three ice-skaters enjoy the frozen shallows near the Causeway, which separates Candlewood Lake and Squantz Pond. (Courtesy of Willie and Hazel Burger.)

ICE-SKATING ON DISBROW'S POND, 1920S. The kids still skate on this pond today, though the farmland in the background is now the Possum Ridge development. (Courtesy of Kenneth Taylor.)

SEA PLANE, 1940S. Ice-skaters line up next to a recently landed sea plane on the frozen waters of Candlewood Lake. (Courtesy of New Fairfield Free Public Library.)

Five

SUNDAYS AND SCHOOL DAYS

BALL POND SCHOOL, EARLY 1900s. Ball Pond School was one of seven one-room schools in town. The school was located on the shore of Ball Pond, not too far from the current intersection of Ball Pond Road and Fairfield Drive. The district for this school included families living on Milltown Road, Titicus Mountain Road, Hudson Drive, Satterlee Road, and Ball Pond Road. The teacher, Alice Ruffles, is standing next to a man who is most likely the school superintendent. (Courtesy of New Fairfield Historical Society.)

BALL POND SCHOOL, EARLY 1900S. Youngsters of the Ball Pond School are wearing high-button shoes, overalls, and black stockings on the boys, while teacher Alice Ruffles dons an apron. In 1803, the school board voted to build a schoolhouse on the west side of Ball Pond. Daniel Hodge built the school for $78. An excerpt from a 1914 Danbury newspaper article states, "One night last week the Balls Pond schoolhouse was completely destroyed by fire. There was no insurance on the building, origin of fire unknown. For the present the school will be continued in a building of Mrs. O.D. Taylor at her home." The rebuilt school finally closed in 1941 and was sold to A. E. Tweedy for $1,800. (Courtesy of New Fairfield Historical Society.)

EAST CENTER SCHOOL, 1915. While the teacher and her students came to school this day dressed in their best, the schoolhouse looks to be in rather sad repair. The small shed portion was probably the wood shed where firewood for the stove was stored. For some years, the parents of the students attending were required to supply a share of the firewood. (Courtesy of New Fairfield Historical Society.)

EAST CENTER SCHOOL IN WINTER, 1919. Students pose for a picture on a "double-ripper" sled. Among these students was Esther Horberg Taylor and Martha Post Fairchild. Notice the sturdy hats, coats, and mittens worn by all. (Courtesy of Kenneth Taylor.)

EAST CENTER SCHOOL, 1938. Donning knickers and pretty dresses, these 23 students pose outside for a picture. The school was moved from the triangle at the intersection of Saw Mill Road and Wood Creek Road to its present location on the opposite side of Saw Mill Road and is now part of a home. In 1941, George M. Nevius purchased the school from the town for $50. (Courtesy of Kenneth Taylor.)

EAST CENTER SCHOOL, 1940. This photograph was taken one year before the Consolidated School opened. The new, large, modern school turned out to be quite a change for the teacher as well as the students. (Courtesy of Willie and Hazel Burger.)

CENTERVILLE SCHOOL, 1903. The Centerville School was located at the bottom of Pine Hill Road and is now part of a home. An 1889 town report shows that $250 was budgeted for this school, including the teacher's salary, books, and supplies. (Courtesy of New Fairfield Historical Society.)

CENTERVILLE SCHOOL STUDENTS, 1935. Most of these boys and girls had quite a walk to school every day. They came from Beaver Bog Road, up Pine Hill Road, and beyond the Methodist church along what is now Route 37. Boys were outnumbered by the girls here, but many wore ties for this special class photograph. (Courtesy of Ruth Kaeser Hawley.)

WOODCREEK SCHOOL, 1930s. What a wonderful teacher Helen Benya Gereg was. She announced, "It is a beautiful day today, let's have school outside!" There were some older male students to carry the desks and chairs outside. Notice the open farmland on the other side of the dirt road. (Courtesy of New Fairfield Historical Society.)

WOODCREEK SCHOOL, 1938. On the shore of Candlewood Lake, this school served families living in the Kellogg Street section of New Fairfield. When the Consolidated School opened, these children either had to be bused around the lake to attend school or pay tuition to Brookfield to go to school there. After many years of controversy, this 450-acre area of New Fairfield was annexed to Brookfield in 1961. (Courtesy of New Fairfield Historical Society.)

INSIDE THE WOODCREEK SCHOOL, 1938. This is a rare view of the inside of one of New Fairfield's one-room schoolhouses. Notice the map of Connecticut on the wall and the radio and daffodils on the teacher's desk. In 1944, the town sold the school for $275 and the land for $200. The schoolhouse was made into a home and still remains on Kellogg Street in Brookfield. (Courtesy of New Fairfield Historical Society.)

BOGUS HILL SCHOOL, C. 1906. Kenneth Joyce, the tall boy in the first row, is one of the students of the Bogus Hill School, also known as the Great Meadow School district. (Courtesy of Agnes Betty Trimpert.)

GREAT MEADOW SCHOOL, 1930S. This schoolhouse was built after the flooding of Candlewood Lake, as the original school of this district was lost to the lake. Town records show that, in 1880, there were 32 students in New Fairfield schools. A teacher's salary in that same year was $26 per month. (Courtesy of New Fairfield Public Library.)

WEST CENTRE SCHOOL, 1940s. Willard Olson was attending the West Centre School when construction began on the new Consolidated School. He recalls that once a week, their teacher, Mrs. Minck, walked her students up to check on the progress of the building. Students went across the dirt road to the Havens home each day for drinking water. (Courtesy of New Fairfield Historical Society.)

LITTLE RED SCHOOLHOUSE, 1970s. In 1970, the newly formed New Fairfield Historical Society was given the West Centre Schoolhouse to restore and use as a museum. The woodshed was moved, and after restoration, the building was painted red. This is the site of the society's annual pumpkin festival. (Courtesy of New Fairfield Historical Society.)

GREAT HOLLOW SCHOOL, EARLY 1900S. This was a very small schoolhouse located in the northwest section of town. In 1883, Katie Kimball was the teacher. This is the only schoolhouse in town that is no longer standing. (Courtesy of New Fairfield Historical Society.)

BASEBALL TEAM AT CONSOLIDATED SCHOOL, 1949. William Delohery, William Jenks, and Joseph Picone are some of the boys waiting for their turn at bat. Uniforms and equipment were not provided, so each player brought his own bat, glove, and talent for a fun game. (Courtesy of New Fairfield Historical Society.)

CONSOLIDATED SCHOOL, 1948. At a 1940 town meeting, $60,000 was approved for construction of the Consolidated School, so called because it brought children from all distances to a central location. The school opened on January 31, 1941, for grades one through eight. Included were four classrooms with two grades in each room, an auditorium, a library, a kitchen, and four activity rooms. The present parking area was a playground at that time. (Courtesy of Willie and Hazel Burger.)

CONSOLIDATED SCHOOL OUTING, 1950s. This group of young students takes a walk along Route 39 in front of the New Fairfield Cemetery with their teacher, Louise Tyler. Notice the absence of the New Fairfield Post Office. (Courtesy of New Fairfield Historical Society.)

FIRST-GRADE PICNIC AT SQUANTZ POND, 1951. This is equivalent to Fun Day, now held each year at the Consolidated School. The students went by bus to Squantz Pond State Park for games, swimming, and a picnic lunch provided by the mothers and the parent-teacher organization. (Courtesy of Karen Schermeister.)

SCHOOL BUS AT CONSOLIDATED SCHOOL, 1950S. Bus driver Gabriel Gillotti brings several students to school. Notice the stacked milk crates set by the side of the building. Several drivers using station wagons made runs throughout town. Hot lunch cost $1 per week back then. (Courtesy of New Fairfield Historical Society.)

EIGHTH-GRADE GRADUATION AT MEETING HOUSE HILL SCHOOL, 1962. Fifty-eight students graduated from the eighth grade in 1962. The girls look lovely with white gloves, flowers, and bouffant hairdos. Boys sported suits and ties and carnations. Until New Fairfield High School opened in 1974, students went to Danbury High School or the Henry Abbott Technical School. (Courtesy of Helen Middleton.)

NEW FAIRFIELD HIGH SCHOOL, 1978. This aerial view of the high school was taken in 1978. Since then, the school has undergone several changes and additions. (Courtesy of New Fairfield Historical Society.)

SIGNING OF BONDING FOR MEETINGHOUSE HILL SCHOOL, 1961. On March 1, 1961, first selectman William Raacke, along with several other town officials, signed the bond to begin the construction of Meeting House Hill School. Since its original construction, the school has been added to four times to accommodate the increasing growth of the town. (Courtesy of New Fairfield Historical Society.)

HIGH SCHOOL GROUND BREAKING, 1972. Onlookers applaud 10 years later as first selcetman Raacke digs in to commemorate the start of construction of a much needed high school in New Fairfield. The school opened its doors in 1974. (Courtesy of Linda Decker.)

NEW FAIRFIELD HIGH SCHOOL BAND, LATE 1970S. This is the band's first uniform, which was purchased used from another high school. Parents of band members formed a group called the Band-Aids to raise money for uniforms and to sew the majorette uniforms. The music director at the time was Alex Thomson. (Photograph by Bob Devine, courtesy of Alex Thomson.)

LUTHERAN CHURCH, 1978. In 1969, the mission of the Lutheran Church of the Good Shepherd was organized. The congregation met at Meeting House Hill School then at the Consolidated School, before property was found to build a church of its own. (Courtesy of New Fairfield Historical Society.)

METHODIST EPISCOPAL CHURCH, EARLY 1900S. The original church was built in 1819. Early in 1835, the congregation decided a larger church was needed. Old church records give the following account: "A house of worship to be built on the same or near the place where the old one stands, not far from thirty by forty feet on the ground, with posts sixteen feet in height, well lighted with an end gallery and thoroughly finished in a workmanlike manner. To be built by Jessie Scudder, Esq." (Courtesy of New Fairfield Historical Society.)

DUTCH REFORMED CHURCH, 1983. This building had many lives as a hotel, church, and private home. When it served the congregation of the Reformed Church of New Fairfield, it was the first affiliate of this denomination in the state of Connecticut. (Courtesy of New Fairfield Historical Society.)

ST. EDWARD'S CHURCH, 1956. In March 1955, ground was broken for the building of St. Edward the Confessor Roman Catholic Church. The first mass in the completed church was held in April 1956. In 2001, a major addition was added to the original church that serves members from New Fairfield and a small part of Danbury. The parish originally included the town of Sherman, but that town now has a church of its own, Holy Trinity Parish, established in 1985. (Courtesy of Preserve New Fairfield, Inc.)

NEW FAIRFIELD FREE PUBLIC LIBRARY, 1962. In 1957, the town purchased the former New Fairfield Congregational Church building to become a library at a cost of $15,000. Originally the library was in the New Fairfield Town Hall and was open on Saturdays from 2:00 p.m. to 4:00 p.m. This converted building served its patrons well, and then an addition was added in 1975. This portion now has the community room (a meeting room), a kitchen, and the New Fairfield Historical Society on the lower level. (Courtesy of Janice Zackeo.)

NEW FAIRFIELD CONGREGATIONAL CHURCH, 1950S. This lovely church was built in 1956 not too far from the site of the very first 18th-century meeting house. It was dedicated on November 17, 1957. The additions of Pilgrim Hall, Sunday school rooms, and a new kitchen were completed in 1968. (Courtesy of New Fairfield Congregational Church.)

CONGREGATIONAL CHURCH WOMEN'S CLUB, 1912. This group of women met regularly at the Horberg home on Woodcreek Road. This organization is still a very supportive part of the church, with some second- and third-generation members involved today. (Courtesy of Kenneth Taylor.)

TOM THUMB WEDDING, 1958. Beautifully dressed young ladies and handsome young men celebrate a Tom Thumb wedding as part of a fund-raiser for the New Fairfield Congregational Church in 1958. (Courtesy of Donald Novicky.)

CAMP MEETING, 1920s. On June 27, 1921, the New Fairfield Congregational Church was struck by lightning and burned to the ground. Many types of fund-raising events were held, and one of these was a camp meeting. This was held near the site of the burned church. The barns in the background were part of the Arthur Chase farm. (Courtesy of Preserve New Fairfield, Inc.)

HORBERG FAMILY PICNIC, 1936. Horberg family members, young and old, meet at Squantz Pond State Park. Doors on the Ford Model A were flung open by eager children, and blankets and baskets of delicious food were carried out to a favorite spot at the park for an afternoon of family, fun, and fireworks. (Courtesy of Kenneth Taylor.)

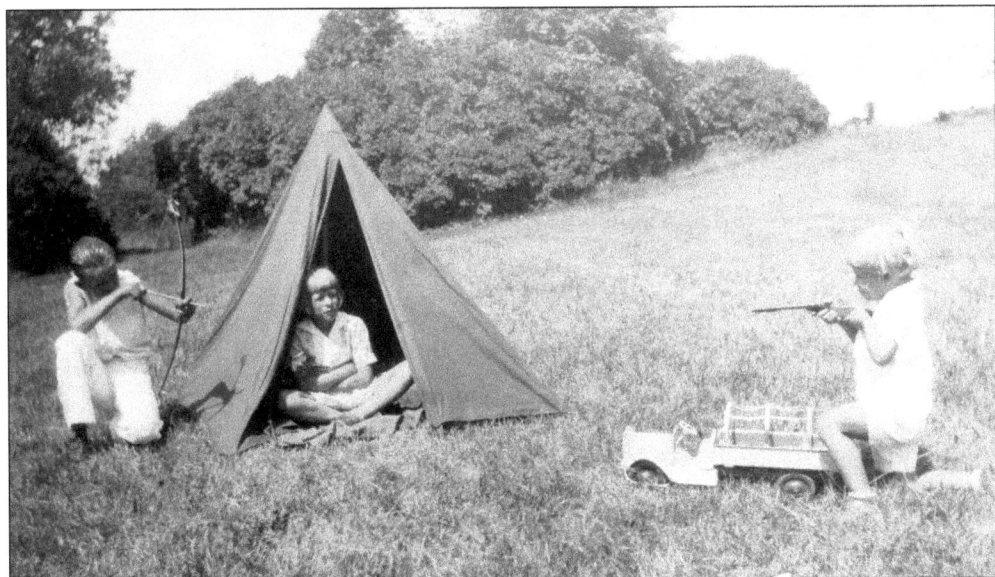

PLAYING "COWBOYS AND INDIANS," 1932. The summer of 1932 finds Alan, Joan, and Doug Muir playing on the lawn by their bungalow on Satterlee Lane. Indeed it was only a lane, as the home sites on Satterlee farm were yet to be built. Arrow Meadow Road and Satterlee Road as they are known today did not exist at the time of this photograph. (Courtesy of John D. and Joan Muir.)

HOMEMADE DOODLEBUG, C. 1937. Here are Gabriel and Peter Gillotti Sr. on the Gillotti farm, which is now the location of the New Fairfield High School. Gabriel's homemade doodlebug vehicle was used for many jobs on the farm. It was a perfect example of "waste not, want not." (Courtesy of Anthony and Marie Gillotti.)

NOT THE *BEVERLY HILLBILLIES,* 1920s. Isabel and Gertrude Johnston, along with some college friends, were headed to Lake Waramaug for a summer vacation. The Johnstons lived on Saw Mill Road, so it was a long trip of about 30 miles. With the automobile jam-packed it is a wonder how the driver got in. (Courtesy of James Green.)

Six

MILESTONES

HAPPY BIRTHDAY, 1944. Birthdays, graduations, weddings, and reunions—these are some of the family moments that make lasting memories. Over the years, the clothing styles and backdrops may have changed, but the joy and warmth of shared time with loved ones remains even today. Eight little friends donned paper hats to celebrate Donald Hatch's seventh birthday in the yard of his family home near Candlewood Corners. This house is listed on the 1867 Beers map of New Fairfield as belonging to G. Cromwell. (Courtesy of Donald and Judy Hatch.)

BABY BUGGY, 1922. Harry Benedict peers out of his wicker carriage on a visit with his grandma Emma Carlson at the Dayton House. Route 37 was still a dirt road. The present-day Neumann Real Estate office is on the left in the background. (Courtesy of Agnes Betty Trimpert.)

LAKE KENOSIA, 1910. Hoping to catch the brass ring, Helen Horton Middleton rides the merry-go-round at this popular amusement park in Danbury. Residents of New Fairfield enjoyed folk dancing, boating, and picnicking here until the park burned down in 1926. (Courtesy of Helen Middleton.)

80

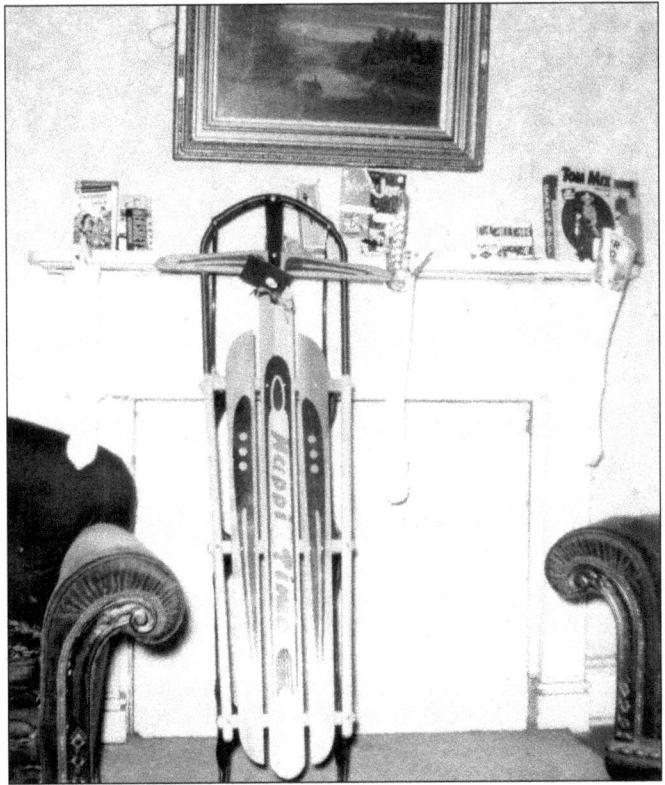

SANTA'S VISIT, 1940S.
Father Christmas left a
sled and a *Tom Mix* book
at the home of Albert
and Antoinette Johnson.
(Courtesy of Richard and
Millie Johnson.)

CONGREGATIONAL CHURCH CONFIRMATION CLASS, 1969. Decked out in white gloves and neckties, these youngsters are confirmands pledging their membership to the church. (Courtesy of John D. and Joan Muir.)

WEDDING RECEPTION AT TOWN HALL, MAY 1938. Newlyweds John and Ada Benedict Urban pose with their friends and family after their wedding reception at the New Fairfield Town Hall. This was a popular place to have a celebration after holding the wedding ceremony next door at the Congregational Church. Note the stone vault and wood pile in the left of the photograph, and the groom (center) wears a jaunty top hat. (Courtesy of Agnes Betty Trimpert.)

RAISING A GLASS TO THE BRIDE AND GROOM, OCTOBER 1946. Rev. Herman DeAnguera (far right), who was the minister of the Congregational Church from 1944 to 1949, makes a toast to Joanne and Harry Moody at their wedding reception held at the Candlewood Knolls clubhouse. The damask tablecloths were family heirlooms. (Courtesy of Harry and Joanne Moody.)

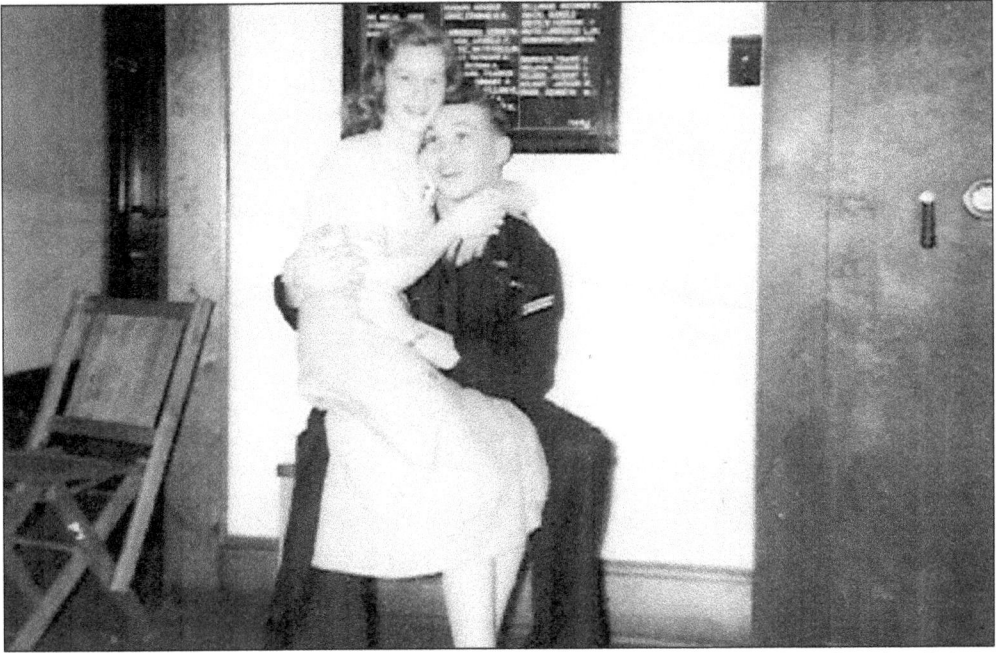

SQUARE DANCING SWEETHEARTS, 1951. Janet Norton and Donald Novicky take a break from the action at a square dance held in the New Fairfield Town Hall. They are sitting near the vault on the lower level. Donald was home on leave from the U.S. Navy radar school. They married in 1953. (Courtesy of Edward Schullery Jr.; courtesy of Donald Novicky.)

JUNE BRIDE, 1947. Rosemary Gillotti and Rick Potenziani pose in front of the bride's home after their wedding. Rosemary and her nine brothers and sisters grew up on the farm that became the high school campus and sports fields. (Courtesy of Anthony and Marie Gillotti.)

FRONT PORCH WEDDING COUPLE, 1930.
Ready to start married life, Esther Horberg
and Kenneth Taylor Sr. leave the Horberg
home on Woodcreek Road on September 21,
1930. Her father, Charles, ran a blacksmith
shop there in the early 1900s. (Courtesy of
Kenneth Taylor.)

WEDDING AT HOME AND FRONT LAWN RECEPTION, 1918. A bouquet of lily of the valley
flowers was picked by Hazel Hatch and tied into love knots for her wedding to Harold Pinckney
on May 18, 1918. Her little cousin Eleanor ponders the duties of the flower girl. Guests enjoyed
the lawn at the Disbrow home on Route 37. (Courtesy of Donald and Judy Hatch.)

ALL SMILES AND SUNDAY BEST, 1951. Friends and family gather for the marriage of Diana Marquis and Ronald Peck. Pictured from left to right are (first row) Robert Peck, Harriet Peck Moissonier, Donna Moissonier Teschioner, Myrtle Carpenter Peck, Diana Marquis Peck, Ida Mallory Peck, Judy Rasmussen Hatch, Clara Peck Rasmussen, Sally Taylor Klatte, and Eva Peck Taylor; (second row) Levi Mallory Peck, David Carpenter Peck, Alfred Moissonier, Ronald Lee Peck, Nancy Moissonier Abdella, Louise Peck Secor, Pat Moissonier Voytek, Nelson Secor, James Rasmussen, and Leonard Taylor. The woman seated behind is unidentified. (Courtesy of Diana Peck.)

CONGREGATIONAL CHURCH WEDDING, 1946. Guests gather for the October 26, 1946, wedding of Joanne Silliman and Harry Moody at the Congregational Church, which now serves as the New Fairfield Public Library community room on the main floor and the New Fairfield Historical Society office in the basement. (Courtesy of Harry and Joanne Moody.)

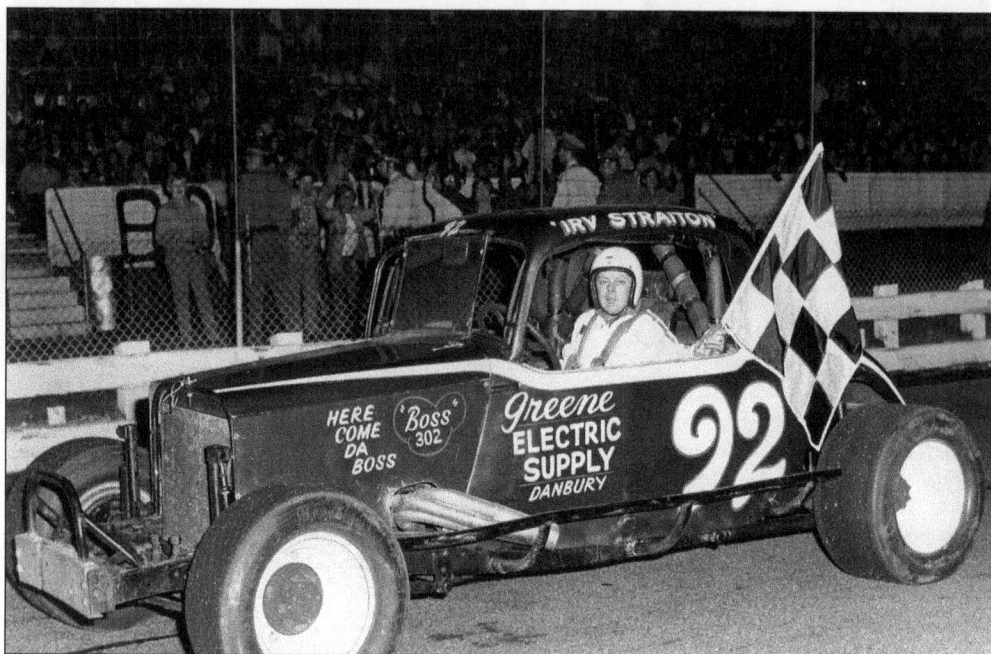

HOT WHEELS, 1969. Irving Straiton drove his stock car at the Danbury Fair race track. He started his racing career in 1969 and always drove No. 92 or No. 93 every Saturday night from April through October. Straiton built his own car and was a member of the Southern New York Racing Association. (Courtesy of Irving Straiton.)

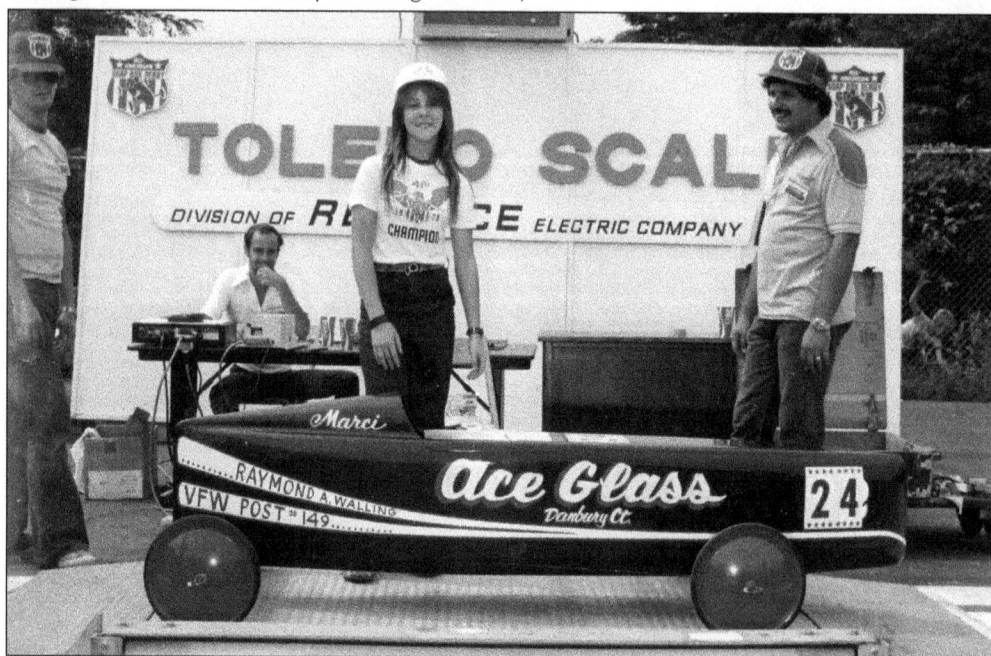

SOAPBOX DERBY RACER, 1977. Marceline (Marci) Straiton was the soapbox derby junior division champion in 1977, senior champion the following year, and went on to compete on the national level. Participants had to build their own car from a kit that included wheels, axels, and cables. (Courtesy of Irving Straiton.)

FAMILY BAND, 1940S. Keeping with the tradition of parties and dances at the town hall, Frances Gillotti (vocals), her brother Anthony (guitar), Ned Watson (banjo), and Jerry Gormeby (accordion) play for the square dancers who were whirling around the floor. The space was located where the present offices of the selectman, tax collector, and assessor are today. Roberta "Ma" Foster said the women served the cake and coffee and the men hid a cider jug outside to "cut the dust from their throats." (Courtesy of Anthony and Marie Gillotti.)

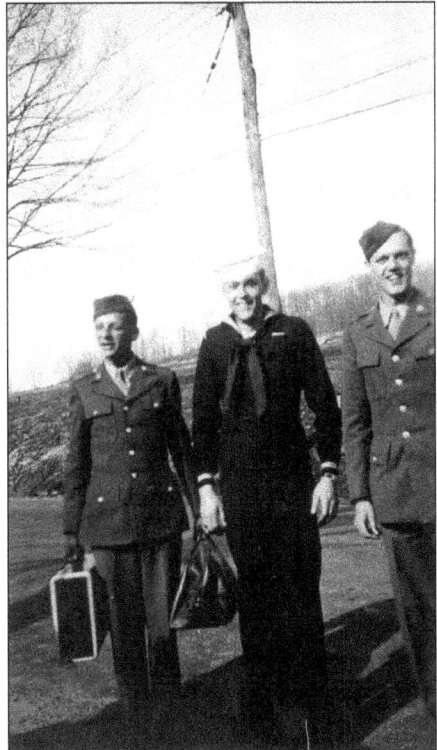

FURLOUGH, 1943. Home on leave from service during World War II, from left to right, Pvt. Freddie Fontaine, Seaman Harry Benedict, and his cousin Pvt. Buddy Joyce reunite in May 1943. Today the New Fairfield Veterans Association maintains a park in the center of town honoring those who served their country from the time of the French and Indian War and the Revolutionary War to present-day conflicts. (Courtesy of Preserve New Fairfield, Inc.)

CAMPSITE AT BODEN'S FIELD, 1941. Fresh air, natural beauty, and the largest lake in Connecticut lured campers, especially folks from New York City. The Burger family returned to this site on Candlewood Lake each year, from 1941 to 1945. (Courtesy of Willie and Hazel Burger.)

HONORING THE PAST, 1961. Testing the Civil War–replica cannon, from left to right, are James Rasmussen, Donald Hatch, Richard Pettibone, first selectman William Raacke, Harvey Johnson, and Charles Fox. It was an annual tradition to fire a cannon at the conclusion of the Fourth of July parade. (Courtesy of Donald and Judy Hatch.)

Seven

FACES

CONIGLIO FAMILY STACKS UP, 1950S. Well-known and well loved in these parts, the Coniglio children enjoyed the playground at the Consolidated School. From bottom to top, they are Patricia, Robert, John, Joseph, Francette, Frank, and Carmella (Millie). (Courtesy of Joseph Coniglio.)

MARTHA POST FAIRCHILD. Martha Post Fairchild (1904–2000) is an important figure in New Fairfield history. One of the few girls to attend high school in Danbury in her time, she also graduated from the Danbury Normal School, now Western Connecticut State University. She is probably best known for her role as librarian for decades. She was one of the original members of the New Fairfield Historical Society and served as town historian for many years. She was a longtime member of the Congregational Church and served as the church school superintendent. She wrote a book, *The Red Rambler Rose*, in which she recalls delightful details of daily life of the early days in New Fairfield. (Courtesy of New Fairfield Historical Society.)

MISS TWIGGLEY'S TREE, 1966. Dorothea Warren Fox, illustrator of Dr. Benjamin Spock's books, magazines, and advertisements on baby and child care, was inspired to write the children's book, *Miss Twiggley's Tree*, by the weeping willow on her property and the tree house occupied by her children. She incorporated local people in the story, which was originally published in 1966 and reprinted in 2002. The tree seen in this Fox family photograph blew down in a storm in 1994, but her story lives on. (Courtesy of New Fairfield Historical Society.)

CHRISTMAS SHOPPING, 1950s. Shopping at holiday time meant ordering from Montgomery Ward's catalog or taking a trip to Woolworth's in Danbury. This photograph shows the Fox children looking over toys as customers enjoy lunch at the fountain counter. (Courtesy of New Fox family.)

DANCING DUO, 1960s. Arriving from New York City in 1956, Al and Connie Fanton ran a "city school in a country setting" by teaching ballet, tap, and ballroom dancing to the young and not-so-young people of the area. A performing couple for decades, the Fantons also wrote, directed, and produced a variety show, *90 Minutes from Broadway*, at the Candlewood Theatre. (Courtesy of Betty Swan.)

SISTERS AND TEACHERS, 1930s. Isabel (left) and Gertrude Johnston sit on the porch of their family home at the top of Saw Mill Hill. Both women graduated from Danbury Normal School (now Western Connecticut State University), were longtime teachers, and were strong advocates for the New Fairfield Free Public Library. (Courtesy of James Green.)

ACTIVE CITIZENS, 1950S. Charles and Mabel Johnson Carlson relax at their home on Route 39 opposite Sweetcake Mountain Road. Charles was a selectman for 27 years, a charter member of the New Fairfield volunteer fire company, the first president of the New Fairfield Lions club, and a well-known contractor specializing in golf courses in his later years. (Courtesy of Richard and Millie Johnson.)

FIVE SCHOOL GIRLS IN A ROW, 1920S. Rose Joyce is pictured second from right in this charming snippet of early-20th-century innocence. (Courtesy of Leonard Copicotto.)

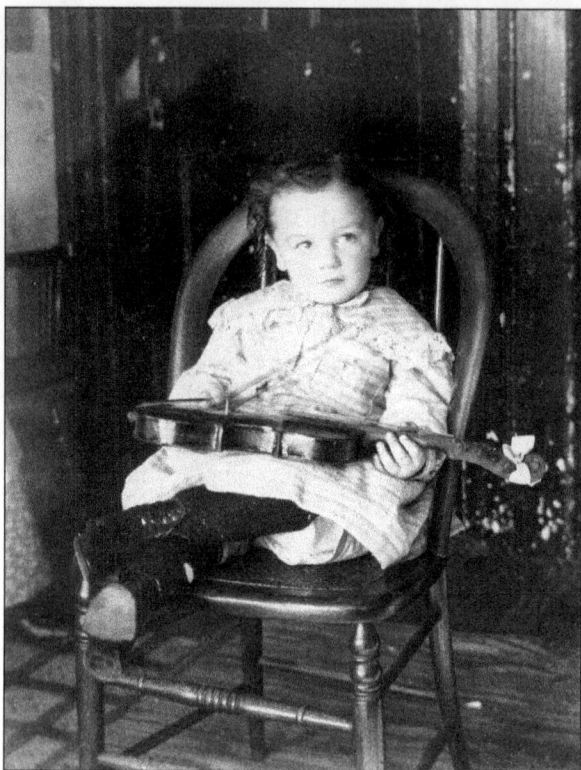

DAD'S FIDDLE, 1899. Kenneth Joyce, age 2, cradles his father's favorite instrument. The family home on Squantz Pond was destroyed when the lake was flooded, but the chimney remained standing and created a hazard for boaters until the 1950s, when it was finally knocked down. (Courtesy of Agnes Betty Trimpert.)

WILLIAM SATTERLEE, 1960S. The name Satterlee has been associated with the Ball Pond area since the Civil War era, when young William Satterlee served as a Connecticut volunteer. His son William (pictured) developed the family farm at Satterlee Lane and gave his name to the road. He also was the proprietor of the Ball Pond Hotel at one time, where the motto was "Services Cheerfully Given." (Courtesy of John D. and Joan Muir.)

HAPPY BIRTHDAY PHEBE, 1912. Phebe Disbrow (third row, left), invited her friend Gladys Carlson (third row, second from left) and her Hatch, Peck, and Disbrow relatives to her birthday party at the family home on the corner of Route 37 and Colonial Road. (Courtesy of Donald and Judy Hatch.)

STRIKING A POSE, 1947. Tossing the bike aside, Francis Miller (left) and Robert Ballard strike a jaunty pose at Candlewood Corners. (Courtesy of Kenneth Taylor.)

TEA PARTY, EARLY 1900S. China cups on a white tablecloth adorn the tiny tea table as Minnie Disbrow pours. Is her imaginary friend late for the party? (Courtesy of Donald and Judy Hatch.)

WAITING FOR THE MAIL, 1915. Phebe Disbrow waits patiently at her home on what is now Route 37. (Courtesy of Harry and Joanne Moody.)

READY FOR WINTER, 1948. Lydia and Peter Gillotti are standing by a supply of firewood at their home on Gillotti Road. Their farm was later sold to the town to build the high school. (Courtesy of Anthony and Marie Gillotti.)

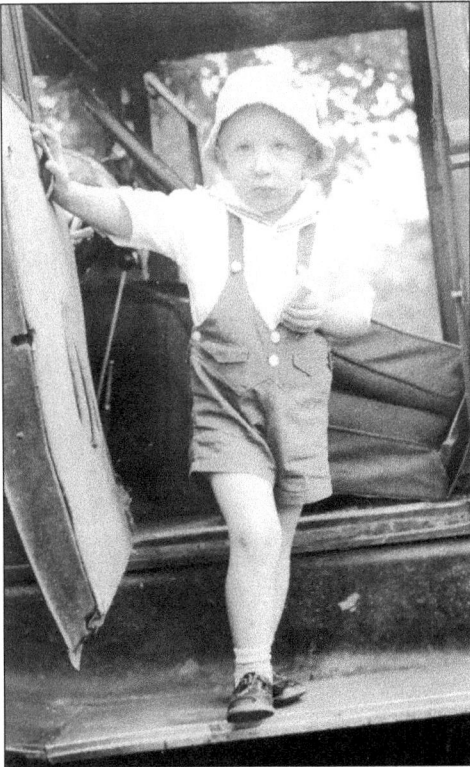

SNACK TIME, 1933. Kenneth Taylor clutches a banana as he steps on the running board of his dad's car. (Courtesy of Kenneth Taylor.)

A SWEET LADY, 1905. Charles A. and Edith Carlson Horberg pose with their son Henry in 1905. They lived in the first house on Woodcreek Road where there was once a blacksmith shop. Edith treated the East Centre School children to homemade cookies as they passed her home at day's end. Her hairpin lace was a coveted gift. (Courtesy of Kenneth Taylor.)

FAMILY PRIDE, 1914. Prominent town families recorded their children in formal portraits, such as this one featuring Hatch family members, from left to right, Ralph, Norris Jr., and Hazel. They lived just beyond Candlewood Corners on the left. Ralph later became a road supervisor and maintained a garage for the Connecticut Department of Transportation. (Courtesy of Donald and Judy Hatch.)

THE HAYES WOMEN, 1924. This was the summer home of the owner of the Tweedy Silk mill, a major employer of New Fairfield residents and supplier of silk bands for Danbury hats. Pictured here at the Tweedy estate on Ball Pond from left to right are Dorothy Hayes Hatch, Elizabeth Hayes Hatch, Margaret Hummel Hayes (mother), Alice Hayes Hoffman, and Hilda Hayes Foley. (Courtesy of Donald and Judy Hatch.)

JOINING FAMILIES, 1918. With ties to the early settlement of New Fairfield and creation of Candlewood Lake, Carrie Chatterton, shown here with her parents, Mary Treadwell and Walter Chatterton, married Keith Joyce. (Courtesy of Leonard Copicotto.)

JANE V. SCHERMERHORN, 1890. Born in 1870 in Schenectady, New York, Jane V. Schermerhorn was a New Fairfield community leader for nearly 50 years. A member of the board of education and active in politics, she first lived in the Henry Orton Leach house on Gillotti Road. When that house burned, she replaced it with a fieldstone structure, which is still standing today. She later resided in a house overlooking Ball Pond, which she ran as a hotel called the Signet Inn. She lived to be 92 years old. Below, Schermerhorn enjoys the sun on her stone house steps in 1915. (Left, courtesy of Linda Decker; below, courtesy of Klaus and Wally Thiel.)

VISITOR TO ANCESTRAL LAND, 1938. Chief Comes with the Dawn (second from left), with an unidentified man (left) and Keith (second from right) and Robert Joyce (right), lives in local lore as an ancestor of Chief Squantz, for whom Squantz Pond is named. (Courtesy of Leonard Copicotto.)

Testimonial

Reception & Dinner

to

Hon. Clarissa E. Nevius

COMMEMORATING THIRTY YEARS OF
SERVICE TO THE TOWN OF NEW
FAIRFIELD IN THE LEGISLATURE
OF THE STATE OF CONNECTICUT

HOTEL GREEN, DANBURY

November, 12 1952

CLARISSA NEVIUS, 1952. In 1952, Clarissa Elwell Nevius was honored with a testimonial dinner to honor "a truly great pioneer for the women's cause in politics in Connecticut." (Courtesy of New Fairfield Historical Society.)

GEORGE NEVIUS, 1900. Known as one half of the couple dubbed, "Mr. and Mrs. New Fairfield," George Nevius was elected in 1911 and served 45 years as town clerk. Active in real estate development, finance, and insurance, he was the first president of the Company A fire department, a director of the Danbury Fair, director of two banks, and a member of the Connecticut General Assembly from 1910 to 1913. Early in his civic career, he was a member of the "Sons of New Fairfield" and helped establish the New Fairfield Free Public Library in 1897. (Courtesy of New Fairfield Historical Society.)

CLARISSA NEVIUS, 1928. Clarissa Elwell Nevius has the distinction of being the first Republican woman elected to the Connecticut General Assembly. She served 30 years, from 1923 to 1953. Her accomplishments included the acquisition of 150 acres to create Squantz Pond State Park, securing electric lines to town, and eliminating a 5¢ toll charge for phone calls between New Fairfield and Danbury. On the home front, she and her husband, George, entertained the townspeople at their annual election day open house, serving oyster stew. (Courtesy of New Fairfield Historical Society.)

LAWN FURNITURE, 1920S. Walter and Mary Treadwell Chatterton enjoy a pleasant afternoon at their home, which is now under Candlewood Lake. Descendents of the couple still own property in this area, called Chatterton Point, and run a popular boat marina there. (Courtesy of Leonard Copicotto.)

GRANVILLE STUBBS, 1930S. Known affectionately as "Stubby," Granville Stubbs was an attorney, journalist, and historian. He lived near Joyceland, maintained an office in Danbury, and was regarded as a whiz at real estate law in his time. (Courtesy of Leonard Copicotto.)

Eight

COMMUNITY SPIRIT

VOLUNTEER FIRE COMPANY, 1948. On November 13, 1934, a group of 39 men met to form the New Fairfield Volunteer Fire Company. The Congregational Cemetery Association agreed to give a site to build a firehouse, providing that the town voted to do it. A town meeting held on October 15, 1935, approved construction of a firehouse at a cost of $3,500. By May 1936, the building was completed. In 1948, Company A purchased the new truck pictured here. Many fund-raisers included dances, minstrel shows, and carnivals. In 1947, a branch of the fire company was formed on Kellogg Street, and further fire protection was provided with the later creation of Squantz Engine Company and Ball Pond Fire Company. In 1982, a new facility was built for Company A, and the original building was renovated for town offices. (Courtesy of New Fairfield Free Public Library.)

FIREMEN'S CHRISTMAS PARTY, 1947. The highlight of the Christmas season in New Fairfield was the Santa Claus party given by the firemen for all of the youngsters in town. This gala event included a Christmas tree, a visit from Santa, and gifts for all the children. (Courtesy of New Fairfield Free Public Library.)

BALL POND VOLUNTEER FIRE COMPANY, 1970s. This company was established on August 2, 1959, to afford fire protection to the Ball Pond area of town and provide help to the entire town where needed. Property on Fairfield Drive was acquired and the building was completed early in 1962. Construction was accomplished entirely by volunteer labor with donations made by the community. This photograph highlights three pieces of Ball Pond Volunteer Fire Company equipment. The trucks pictured here, from left to right, are a 1947 American LaFrance, a 1973 Dodge Pumper, and a 1970 International Tanker. (Courtesy of New Fairfield Historical Society.)

SQUANTZ ENGINE COMPANY, 1958. In 1958, the residents of the Squantz Pond area formed their own fire district and acquired land from the state in 1959 on which to build a firehouse. The original three bay, single-story station was built by the members. At the same time, they acquired their first piece of equipment, a used 1942 Cadillac ambulance, which was temporarily parked next door at the Green Light Restaurant. A second story was added to the building in 1972. (Courtesy of Willie and Hazel Burger.)

NEW FAIRFIELD VOLUNTEER FIRE COMPANY, 1936. Members gathered in March 1936 to inspect the first apparatus purchased by the company, a Ford truck with a front-mounted pump. Kenneth Taylor Sr. is behind the wheel and Rudolph Behrens stands nearby. Today the truck is used as a parade wagon. (Courtesy of Kenneth Taylor.)

THE ORIGINAL POP WARNER CHEERLEADERS, 1970. This group of smiling girls were the first Pop Warner cheerleaders in town. The team included Candy Kipp, Leesa Hawley, Joann Ingram, Susan Dunham, Dianne Pracuta, Liz Ahlrichs, Debbie Kilcourse, Cassie Dunham, Vickee Hawley, Miss Hooper, Donna Sklenar, and Cara Ahlrichs. More than 30 years later, the New Fairfield Falcon Pop Warner cheerleaders took home first-place trophies from national competitions. (Courtesy of Barbara Coelho.)

LITTLE LEAGUE TEAM, 1978. The New Fairfield Lions club has sponsored many baseball teams since it was organized in 1951. These boys were members of the Orange Major team, pictured with coaches Michael Hess (left) and Michael Gillotti. (Courtesy of Michael Hess.)

BROWNIE MEETING TODAY, 1953. This Brownie troop held its meetings at the New Fairfield Town Hall and worked on earning many badges while belonging to the oldest organization for young girls, the Girl Scouts of America. (Courtesy of Karen Schermeister.)

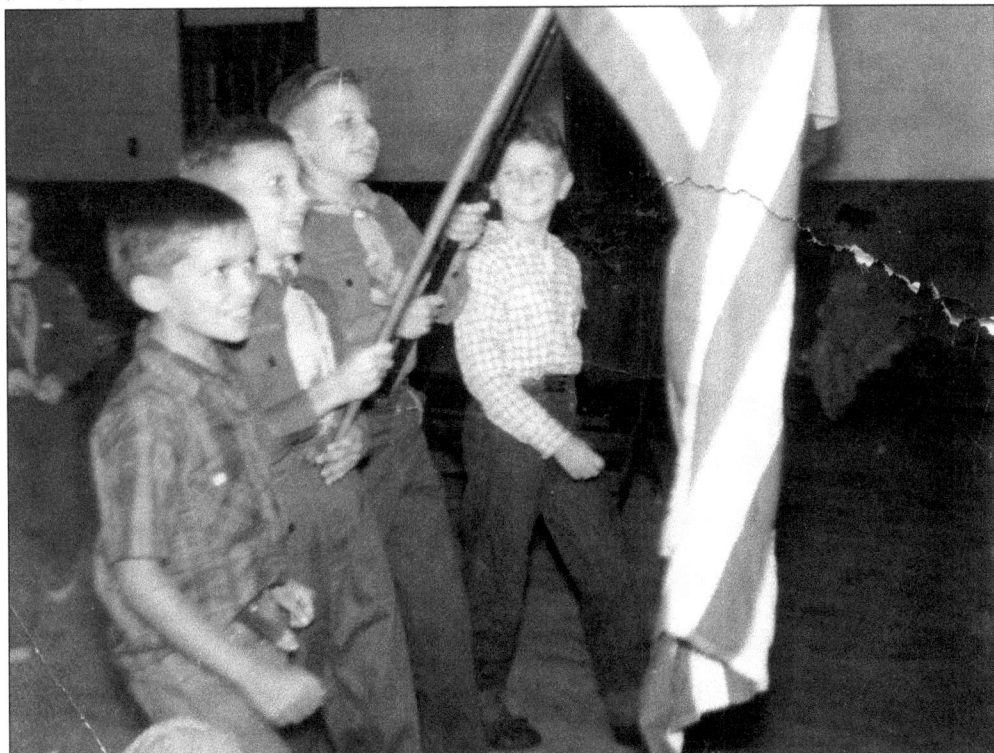

SMILING PLEDGE, 1955. A dedicated group of young men salute the flag during a Cub Scout meeting at the New Fairfield Town Hall. (Courtesy of Helen Middleton.)

4-H CLUBS, 1945. In 1914, 4-H clubs were founded for children, ages 9 to 19, to help farm youth learn by doing. The name is taken from its emblem, a four-leaf clover with an H on each leaf, which stands for head, hands, heart, and health. In New Fairfield, 4-H clubs were active until the 1970s and sometimes numbered as many as five different clubs. This photograph features several New Fairfield girls who attended a state convention in Storrs. (Courtesy of New Fairfield Historical Society.)

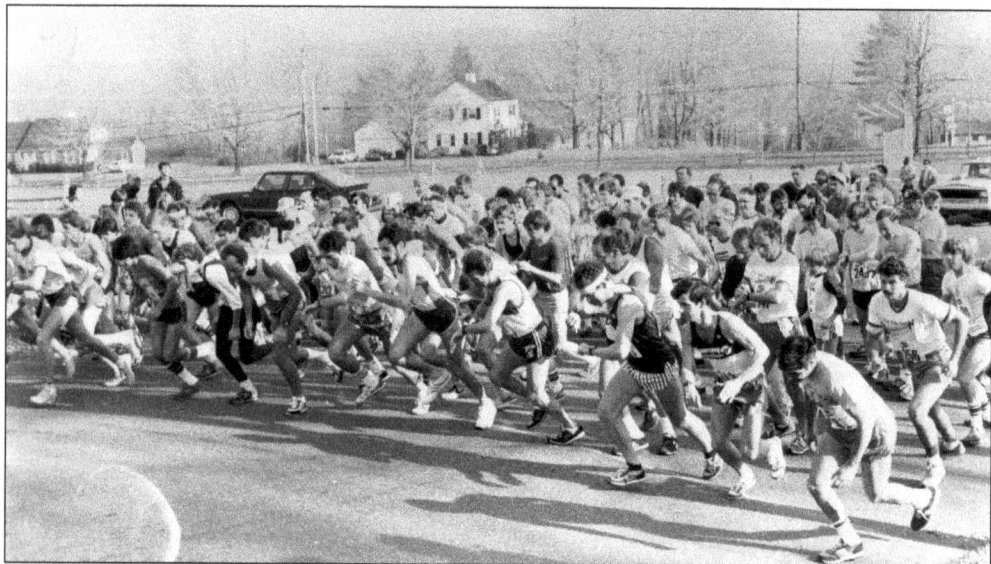

RUN FOR THE TURKEYS, 1970S. The starting line for the Run for the Turkeys was at the Consolidated School parking lot years ago, but now it all starts at the high school. Sponsored by New Fairfield Parks and Recreation, this is an annual five kilometer race open to all runners in mid-November. Winners go home with a turkey, of course. (Courtesy of New Fairfield Parks and Recreation.)

110

AIRBORNE, 1975. Imagine the New York Jets professional basketball team here in New Fairfield in a matchup against members of the Lions club. The fund-raiser was held on March 9, 1975, at Meeting House Hill School. Tickets were $2.50 for adults and $1.50 for children under 12. This action photograph shows No. 52, Steve Reese, of the Jets and Michael Hess (in white shorts) of the Lions going for a jump ball. (Courtesy of Michael Hess.)

UNDEFEATED, 1964–1965. This is the New Fairfield Parks and Recreation senior basketball team that had a perfect season of nine wins. From left to right are (first row) Ronald Johnson, James Flynn, Joseph Coniglio, and David Goelz; (second row) Robert Coniglio, John Taggart, Henry Janssen, and coach Michael Hess. (Courtesy of Michael Hess.)

LEAGUE OF THEIR OWN, 1969. The ladies of the Congregational Church had their own bowling league and played at the Holiday Bowl in Brookfield. From left to right are Sandra Norton, Karen Schermeister, Luella Norton, Janet Novicky, and Jeanette Schroeder. (Courtesy of Donald Novicky.)

MEN'S BOWLING LEAGUE, 1965. Brothers, friends, and fellow church members bowled together for many years. From left to right are (first row) Downing Middleton and Orin Bass; (second row) John Middleton, William Fenwick, and Kenneth Bass. (Courtesy of Michael and Dotty Hess.)

GOLDEN FLAMES DRUM CORPS, 1970S. Formed by the Silvestri family for all New Fairfield children, the group practiced at the family's home on Middleton Drive. Original uniforms came used from a church in Manhattan and the group marched in the St. Patrick's Day parade in New York City. (Courtesy of Preserve New Fairfield, Inc.)

FIFE, DRUM, AND BUGLE CORPS, 1971. The corps was founded by the New Fairfield Volunteer Fire Company. The corps was directed by William Burger, and Frank Tully was corps officer. More than 80 youngsters ranging in age from 10 to 18 applied, though many had never played an instrument before. Its first parade was on Memorial Day 1972 in Sherman. The corps is pictured here in full-dress uniform, all homemade. (Courtesy of Willie and Hazel Burger.)

TOWN TALENT, 1947. In 1946 and 1947, friends and neighbors came together to blend their talents for a minstrel show held at the Consolidated School. The first year, the event was sponsored by the parent-teacher association of the Consolidated School and New Fairfield Volunteer Fire Company A. The second year, it was sponsored only by the fire department. It is hard to tell if the cast or the audience had more fun at this raucous fund-raising event. (Courtesy of Joyce Czudak.)

FANTONS' 90 MINUTES FROM BROADWAY, 1967. Created by Connie and Al Fanton as a building fund-raiser for the New Fairfield Congregational Church, the first show was held in June 1967 at the Candlewood Theatre (formerly the Meadowbrook Playhouse). Sponsored by the Church Service Club, this annual production was a social highlight for many years. Scores of local adults and teens put on makeup and costumes in order to be stars once a year. Shows mimicked current and past events, including the age of Aquarius to the Wild West, "where men were men and women were glad of it." (Courtesy of Agnes Betty Trimpert.)

Nine

HOUSES

PARSONAGE, 1950S. Noted on the 1867 Beers map of New Fairfield as the home of A. F. Beardsley, it was purchased by the Congregational Church in 1903 as a home for the parson and his family. For decades, this building was the scene of many church social events and Sunday school meetings. Located in the center of town on old Route 37 behind what was the Congregational Church (now the New Fairfield Free Public Library), the house was privately owned from 1960 to 2007, when it was given to the town and moved intact to a new location just a few hundred yards up the road. Known again as the parsonage, it serves the town as a local history museum and home to Preserve New Fairfield, Inc. (Courtesy of New Fairfield Free Public Library.)

SAWMILL NAMESAKE, 1900. Saw Mill Road is named for this building that sits in the hollow next to Ball Pond Brook. Over the years, it served as a true sawmill, a carding mill, and is today a private residence. (Courtesy of New Fairfield Free Public Library.)

WHEELER HOUSE, 1867. Likely built long before it was noted on the 1867 Beers map of New Fairfield, this home was owned by G. W. Wheeler, who worked as a wool carder and fur picker. Later it became known as "the house by the side of the road" and did a turn as a tea house in the 1930s. It is located on Saw Mill Road just above the old sawmill. (Courtesy of New Fairfield Free Public Library.)

116

Rowley House, 1920s. This little house, noted on the 1867 Beers map of New Fairfield as belonging to G. Whitlock, sits on a ledge near Candlewood Lake at the end of Woodcreek Road, which probably explains how it escaped the flooding. Martha Post Fairchild and Mamie Rowley were childhood friends, and Fairchild recalled attending a sewing bee there. (Courtesy of New Fairfield Free Public Library.)

Scudder Home, 1867. Descendents of the original Scudder family, listed as owners of this home on the 1867 Beers map of New Fairfield, were still living in the house into the 1950s. Isaac Scudder, born in 1803, became the minister of the nearby Methodist Church in 1833. (Courtesy of New Fairfield Free Public Library.)

HOME OF MARSHALL TREADWELL, 1940S. Easily recognizable today, this beautiful, old home sits on Route 39 across from the Company A firehouse. On the 1867 Beers map of New Fairfield, it is designated as belonging to A. Brush. In the 1930s and 1940s, Marshall Treadwell lived here. He was very active in town affairs and served as town treasurer. (Courtesy of New Fairfield Free Public Library.)

THE FARM HOUSE, 1940S. When Candlewood Lake was created, many farms and homes were lost. This house, however, which belonged to the Disbrow family, managed to survive. Today it is part of the Candlewood Knolls community and is referred to as "the farm house." For years it contained a store, and this 1947 photograph shows a sign on the corner of the porch indicating a phone inside. (Courtesy of New Fairfield Free Public Library.)

PINE HILL SENTRY, 1947. This charming little house looks pretty much the same as it has for decades. Likely built before 1867, it was owned by Mrs. Edison Elwell at the time of this photograph. When she lived here, the house was surrounded by farmland. Today it is surrounded by houses. (Courtesy of New Fairfield Free Public Library.)

ERNEST AND ABBI BENEDICT HOME, 1915. Abbi Benedict and some lady friends relax on the porch of her Bear Mountain Road home after the wash was hung to dry. Note the trousers hanging on line in left foreground. The left portion is the original house built in the 1700s. Ernest, a blacksmith and carpenter, built the addition around 1900. The property included a blacksmith shop, a barn, pig pens, a chicken coop, and a frog pond. Much of the meadows was sold to develop Chestnut Hill and Sleepy Hollow in the 1950s. (Courtesy of Agnes Betty Trimpert.)

ORCHARD RIDGE, 1947. This house dates back to the 1700s. The name Orchard Ridge invokes the image of it nestled among apple trees pink with spring blossoms. In the 1930s and 1940s, the Hilbert Heuer family lived there. On the 1867 Beers map of New Fairfield, it was owned by C. Treadwell. Recent owners have meticulously restored the old gem and found some initials carved in the barn attic. (Courtesy of New Fairfield Free Public Library.)

CHARCOAL RUN, 1930s. Originally owned by town clerk E. M. Beers, this house was also home to LeGrand Hopkins, who became the first mayor of Danbury. In the 20th century, the place was purchased by well-known artists Darrel and Margot Austin. This site is also famous as the spot where the legendary battle of Charcoal Run was fought. It has been said that men from Danbury had come to tear down a peace flag raised by New Fairfielders during the Civil War. The story goes that the local boys fought them off with pitchforks. (Courtesy of New Fairfield Free Public Library.)

DUNLAVEY HOME, 1900. This house is shown on the 1867 Beers map of New Fairfield and at that time was probably only a portion of what is shown in this picture. It is believed to have been built between 1825 and 1830. Daniel Dunlavey purchased the home in 1870 for $250. It still stands today and can be seen on Route 39 on the way to the town beach on Candlewood Lake. (Courtesy of New Fairfield Free Public Library.)

JOHN HOYT HOUSE, 1948. This shingled farmhouse, still standing today, was built by John Hoyt, who is credited with building several other houses in town. This is his homestead on the 1867 Beers map of New Fairfield. The farm originally included 50 acres and an apple orchard. At that time, Titicus Mountain Road was an important route to Danbury. In the 1950s, the place was known as Locust Hill Farm, which was a poultry farm with eggs delivered by William Raacke in his station wagon. (Courtesy of Linda Decker.)

KELLOGG HOUSE, 1885. The Kellogg family put on their best "bib and tucker," and brought out the prize horses and even the dog to pose in front of this stately homestead. The house still stands on Kellogg Street, now in Brookfield. Before Candlewood Lake was created, this was actually part of New Fairfield's Woodcreek district. The family owned a slave, Phillis, buying her when she was just two years old. She is buried with the family in the New Fairfield Cemetery in the center of town. (Courtesy of Ken Kellogg.)

LOCUST GLEN, 1906. There are not many people who can say they are the fourth generation to be living in the family homestead. Yet this is true of Daniel and Marion Gerow, who currently live on this former dairy farm located in the Great Hollow district of town. In its heyday, the farm also included a sawmill and icehouse. The Gerow family was one of the earliest to live in New Fairfield and has always been active in community affairs. They are original members of the New Fairfield Historical Society and longtime members of the Congregational Church. (Courtesy of New Fairfield Free Public Library.)

BALL POND HOTEL, 1920S. William Satterlee built the hotel on Ball Pond in the early 1920s, intending to provide New Yorkers with good bathing, boating, and fishing. Guests were met at the Danbury train for a vacation promising "pure air." Outfitting the rooms cost $30 for a mahogany dresser; 22 porch rockers were ordered at $2.25 each. Later known as the Hahlawah Hotel, it was named for the Native American medicine man believed to have lived nearby. It was also called Edgemere when it was owned by returning World War II veterans, who purchased it for $18,500. It was later resold, slated for demolition, and saved by the Dutch Reformed Church. It is now a private residence. (Courtesy of New Fairfield Free Public Library.)

HORBERG HOME, 1936. This beautiful home was once owned by the Hawley family, who operated a wagon factory there in the late 1800s. Later Charles Horberg had a blacksmith shop here. (Courtesy of Kenneth Taylor.)

THIS PLACE FOR SALE, 1947. Walter Czudak sits in the shade of a maple wondering who will purchase this country home. No fancy advertising was used here, just a name and a number to call. (Courtesy of Czudak family.)

ONLY THE STEPS REMAIN, 1940. The weathered, shingled Miller house, near the corner of Milltown Road and Route 39, burned in 1947. The stone steps, however, remained to welcome the owners of the new residence built here. (Courtesy of Lloyd Decker.)

SQUANTZ POND RANGER HOME, 1900S. Today a similar building stands on the same site as this home built by B. Wildman before 1867. Later it was home to Nicholas Rech, who was the first ranger for Squantz Pond State Park. His son George took over the job and retired in 1971. (Courtesy of New Fairfield Free Public Library.)

DAWSON HOUSE, BUILT 1750–1800. Originally owned by G. Jennings, this home was later owned by Walter Dawson, who was a town selectman in 1926. His wife was active in the Red Cross in 1928 and their daughter Margaret attended the Centreville School. (Courtesy of New Fairfield Free Public Library.)

MEMORY LANE, EARLY 1800s. This photograph, taken prior to the 1867 fire that claimed the center building, features some very important early structures, some of which are still standing today. At the bottom of Saw Mill Road, the building on the left is part of Hatch's sawmill. Across the street is the home and store of town clerk E. M Beers, where the town records were destroyed by fire. On the right is the home of another town clerk, LeGrand Hopkins, a hat maker, who moved to Danbury and became its first mayor. This property is credited for being the scene of the battle of Charcoal Run. (Courtesy of New Fairfield Historical Society.)

JOHNSTON HOME ON SAW MILL ROAD, 1900s. Surrounded by pristine land, the George Johnston home at the crest of Saw Mill Road enjoyed far-reaching views west to Brookfield and south to Danbury. The Birches, New Fairfield's first condominium complex, was built on this property without destroying the original farm house. (Courtesy of James Green.)

NEW FAIRFIELD INN, 1940. This house was at one time an inn offering rest and relaxation to travelers. The grounds included a pond and brook. Today the pond no longer exists, as the water has been piped under the road. The 1867 Beers map of New Fairfield shows the A. R. Stevens fur shop on this site. (Courtesy of Linda Decker.)

ON THE MOVE, 1950S. Seen moving along Gillotti Road in the 1950s, a truck pulls a structure. What is it? A vintage schoolhouse? A family-size Chick Sales privy? A playhouse for the kids? Perhaps Grandma stayed too long? (Courtesy of Anthony and Marie Gillotti.)

ACROSS AMERICA, PEOPLE ARE DISCOVERING SOMETHING WONDERFUL. *THEIR HERITAGE.*

Arcadia Publishing is the leading local history publisher in the United States. With more than 3,000 titles in print and hundreds of new titles released every year, Arcadia has extensive specialized experience chronicling the history of communities and celebrating America's hidden stories, bringing to life the people, places, and events from the past. To discover the history of other communities across the nation, please visit:

www.arcadiapublishing.com

Customized search tools allow you to find regional history books about the town where you grew up, the cities where your friends and family live, the town where your parents met, or even that retirement spot you've been dreaming about.

9 7 8 1 5 3 1 6 3 6 5 9 3